# HOW TO RUN A
# STREET SMART
# NONPROFIT!

## 10 Success
### "Secrets" from
### Street Smart
### Leaders

POWER
CIRCLES
80/20
RULE
ELEVATOR
SPEECHES
BOTTOM UP
PLANNING

# DR. WILLIAM MINDAK
## Contributions by CATHERINE M. LENIHAN

ISBN: 1466479981

ISBN-13: 9781466479982

Library of Congress Control Number: 2011919788
CreateSpace Independent Publishing Platform
North Charleston, South Carolina

# ACKNOWLEDGEMENTS

Dr. William A. (Bill) Mindak has spent most of his academic career either starting up nonprofits or helping them become more business-like and Street Smart in their operations. He was the first Director of the Tulane Business School Executive MBA program. He has served as a consultant to Tulane's Medical Center, the Volunteers of America, Credit Union National Association (CUNA), and the Lighthouse of the Blind. He's published articles on applying Marketing to the March of Dimes and to professional practices. He's conducted workshops for the American Heart Association, the American Lung Association, and the Volunteers of America. Currently he's working with the Odyssey House of Louisiana and the Wellness Center of Louisiana. He is Professor Emeritus of Marketing at the A. B. Freeman School of Business and consultant to the Goldring International Institute.

Catherine Lenihan has made important contributions to this book. She is on the faculty of Delgado Community College and an adjunct instructor at Tulane University.

The author wishes to thank Dr. Monique DeKermadec for her words of encouragement and inspiration.

# CHAPTER    TABLE OF CONTENTS    PAGE

# LISTING OF CASES:

# PREFACE
# WHY A BOOK ABOUT STREET SMARTS
# FOR NON PROFITS?

In working with scores of nonprofit executives, I've found many who are good at managing day-to-day operations. Some are excellent fund raisers and rainmakers. Some are good cheerleaders and politicians. But the ones that seem to show steady growth no matter their size are what I call Street Smart Leaders. The dictionary defines street smarts as a combination of practical skills and attitude to strive (and thrive) in difficult or dangerous situations

Street Smart Leaders seem to defy conventional wisdom (it's too conventional and not particularly wise).

For example:
- They realize that even nonprofits have to be "profit-able" - - i.e. mutually beneficial to all parties concerned;
- They grow from the inside out rather than the outside in - - growth is organic;
- They do planning from the bottom up and marketing from the top down
- They <u>focus</u> on the Vital Few people who share in the Vision of their nonprofit and buy totally into the belief

of what makes their nonprofit truly different; (the 80/20 Rule).

- They <u>really listen</u> to the people they serve and talk less about WHAT they do and more about WHY they do it (Shared relations and Beliefs).
- They seem to "know" intuitively how to minimize the impact of change and coach the right people to respond to it. After all since the mission of their nonprofit is to help others change why not their own organization?
- They take advantage of being <u>small</u> so that they can be more flexible and respond faster to competitors. Their limited resources are merely a challenge to do what they do best but to do it better. Their primary job is Chief Hurdle Removing Officer.
- Finally they realize that street smart leadership does not reside in any one person. It is a collective process that is spread through networks of people —donors, clients, volunteers, staff members. If <u>they</u> get what they want, the nonprofit gets what <u>it</u> wants. Everyone does marketing!

The problem with learning to be street smart is that this practical intelligence is not, or perhaps cannot, be taught in business schools. Few textbooks seem to even recognize the concept. Curiously the Leaders with this talent seem to just take it for granted, see nothing special in their abilities and rarely share their "secrets". Like skilled artists or musicians they just seem to "know."

And so this is why I've created this book. I've pulled together some of their best practices, their so-called "secrets" and their tips as to how to run more successful operations. They've also offered insights and recommendations for the exciting future that faces nonprofits.

In addition I've added specific cases to illustrate these practices, some of my own personal experiences in working with nonprofits, and practical exercises so that readers can apply these concepts to their own organization.

According to the Congressional Research Service, in 2009 nonprofits were a $1.40 trillion industry with over 1.5 million nonprofits ranging from healthcare to social assistance. They employed 12.9 million people representing over 10% of the American workforce. Unfortunately, over a million of these nonprofits are under $500,000 in annual revenue and need to grow.

It is to this group of nonprofits that this book is especially dedicated. The key here is to understand that a small nonprofit is just not a small BIG nonprofit. It has special needs, resources and culture. It can benefit most from an injection of Street Smarts.

# PART I
# OVERVIEW

# CHAPTER 1

# FACTS OF LIFE FOR NONPROFITS. SOME GOOD NEWS AND SOME NOT SO GOOD. BE WARY OF LIFE CYCLE THINKING

**"Never doubt that a small group of committed people can change the world. It is the only thing that ever has"**

**Margaret Mead**

Let's start with good news first.

Nonprofits in the US rank third in the service industries after wholesaling and retailing in their importance to our economy and 30,000 new nonprofits are created each year. Some 1.5 million nonprofits have resources (financial and in-kind) that make it a $1.40 trillion industry! They have considerable clout with national and local governments, as well as key businesses which means considerable support for networking, public-private partnerships and strategic alliances.

A recent report from Public Agenda shows that communities deeply value and appreciate their local nonprofits and the services they provide. Donors and volunteers for the most part are passionate and positive about their nonprofits. Their contributions of time and money are based on personal experience, emotional connections, and a sense of deep loyalty.

The spirit of volunteerism in the United States continues unabated. Demographic trends on the age spectrum suggest a huge supply of volunteers, board members and potential donors looking for an elevated purpose in life and the opportunity to do well by doing good.

There is a whole new breed of volunteers - - baby boomers and retirees with time, expertise and ideas, looking for community based projects and humanitarian activities. Nonprofits provide a chance to practice entrepreneurial/management skills without personal financial risk. Research indicates that these "young retirees" tend to be more positive, more patient and have more problem-solving skills than volunteers from previous generations.

Lastly, we have young people getting more involved in social activism and human rights through service learning. As an example, Tulane University, after Hurricane Katrina, established an undergraduate program in which all students must take two courses integrating community service projects with classroom learning as a requirement for graduation. There are scores of other colleges and even K-12 schools interested in using what they have learned in the classroom to solve real-life problems.

Along with this development is the growth of "social entrepreneurship" that calls for a "double bottom-line focus"- - applying business and investment strategies to financial performance with positive social impact. Leading universities have now established chairs in social entrepreneurship with institutes and programs teaching the approach to maximize profits <u>and</u> social responsibility. The conventional separation between the government sector, the private sector and the "third sector" is blurring. It is not unusual among some of the larger nonprofits to find that they are attracting more money through grants and foundations than they are from conventional donations. The private sector is increasingly funding the third sector through strategic alliances, co-branding, and shared causes and public relations activities. Nonprofits often serve as intermediaries as well as recipients.

Nonprofits now have instantaneous communication and emerging technologies that provide potential for shared appeals, cooperative boards, and interactive networks. Social media are used by groups of individuals or organizations to create leaderless movements that could not have been done before. The new connected world offers nonprofits opportunities to get information instantly. They can locate expert help and secondary research data or go online for contacts, introductions and shared experiences and missions. Nonprofits are no longer constrained by brick and mortar facilities - - they can operate their nonprofits virtually everywhere.

Now, the "<u>not so good news</u>".

In real estate they say its Location, Location, and Location. For nonprofits it's Competition, Competition, and Competition! It's not only competition for funding sources, but for attracting volunteers, board members and staff. Unfortunately this competition is not evenly distributed. Some 3000 nonprofits are launched every month. Of those 1.5 million nonprofits we mentioned, almost 1.2 million have annual revenues of less than $500,000. While the media frequently feature large foundations and organizations, from the Bill and Melinda Gates Foundation to the American Cancer

Society, the vast majority of nonprofits are not much larger than "mom and pop" grocery stores. Limited resources, human and financial, seem to be the order of the day.

Nonprofits at one time normally worked in areas where the Public Sector (Government) or the Private Sector (Business) did not want to or could not go. Now competition is not just from other nonprofits. It is also with for profit companies and political parties who have gotten into the act..Their nonprofits provide an impartial sounding platform for their points of view and they come armed with huge war chests, sophisticated marketing and advertising agencies and integrated marketing communications. At no time in our history have there been more special pleaders and "noisemakers" competing for the public's attention, time and money.

Research has documented confusion among the public as to what constitutes a nonprofit. Consumers wonder how hospitals and universities with their "outrageous" fees can be considered nonprofits. This confusion is compounded by many nonprofits selling products, offering services and charging fees to supplement donations. For many people there are just too many appeals using slick web pages, sophisticated annual reports, and telemarketing and call centers to solicit donations.

## The Recession that won't go away!

Although the recession has officially ended, many nonprofits are still struggling to meet their needs. Many Foundations and funders are taking a wait and see approach to giving that depends on the stock market's roller coaster performance. Consistent contributors seem more concerned about themselves in today's economy – replete with high unemployment, real estate foreclosures, battles in Congress over taxes and the country's looming debt - than they are in helping others. Many volunteers find that they have to devote more time to earning a living.

The "Giving USA" annual report points out that the small to medium-sized charities are still trying to get back to 2001 annual revenues. Contributions as a percent of Gross National Product are down to 2% from a high of 2.3% in 2001.

We have talked about nonprofits in general, so now let's identify who the Leading Players in contributions are by market share according to the "Giving USA" report of 2012:

| | |
|---|---|
| Religion | 32% |
| Education | 13% |
| Human services | 12% |
| Gifts to grant making Foundations | 9% |
| International Affairs | 8% |
| Health | 8% |
| Public society, benefit | 7% |
| Arts and culture, humanities | 4% |
| Environment and animals | 3% |
| Gifts to individuals | 1% |
| Unallocated | 3% |
| Total 2011 contributions: $298.42 (billions) | |

Along with these external factors, one of the biggest problems is the DISCONNECT between what many nonprofits DO and what they actually ACHIEVE. These disconnects seem to have four internal causes:

- <u>Increasing size</u>. While there is nothing wrong with getting bigger to take advantage of economies of scale, often this becomes a goal in itself - the "we're number one" syndrome. But with growth comes increased complexity and bureaucracy. Drucker calls this "organized chaos". There is increasing friction between boards and management; volunteers and paid staff; smaller donors and those seeking larger grants, etc. With many layers, plans coming from "on high" find difficulties in execution. Managers seem to spend an inordinate time in managing and not in leading the nonprofit toward its goal.

- <u>Success</u>. Surprisingly, a nonprofit's success may cause a problem. With increasing size usually comes a change in the mix of financial support. Larger nonprofits rely on money from foundations, corporations, state and local governments and less on a broad mix of individuals from the local economy. This changes the culture of the nonprofit. There are new voices to listen to; new criteria for performance. Some nonprofits may start taking their original funders and core groups for granted and may even neglect them. With success, the mission gets broadened or even changed with too many options and choices. Ironically, the nonprofit may eliminate the programs that made it successful in the first place.

- <u>Overdependence on the charismatic leader</u>. Often it is the founder or leader's vision for the nonprofit that drives momentum for early growth. But charismatic leaders rarely build charismatic organizations. Once they leave or get bored, there is no system established to sustain the organization or carry on the mission.

- <u>The unwillingness and reluctance to sell or market themselves</u>. Or as one board member said - - "using the tools of the devil," Simply put marketing is everything that a nonprofit does to grow and that does <u>not</u> necessarily mean costly advertising or promotion. Everyone therefore who works with or for a nonprofit –board member, volunteer, staff or donor -is really a marketer. One can use euphemistic names – rainmakers, outreach specialists, communications directors- but it is all about marketing <u>and</u> selling. As Thomas Watson, CEO of IBM said often:"Nothing happens until someone sells something."

# FUNDAMENTAL DIFFERENCES BETWEEN FOR PROFITS AND NONPROFITS

| For Profits | Nonprofits |
|---|---|
| GOALS/VALUES | |
| Monetary profit is primary purpose | "Social" profit is primary purpose |
| Would eliminate functions, people, activities not contributing to profit | Often keeps functions, programs, and people even if not profitable |
| Single Bottom Line | Many Bottom Lines |
| | |
| RESOURCES | |
| Potentually unlimited- competitive nature limits cooperation legal and tax restrictions | Limited financial, but can trade time and materials, Tax incentives - subject to review |
| Would cease to exist if company consumed more resources than it produces | Could continue to operate if not profitable |
| Economies of scale / scope | Economies of scale limited |
| Global opportunities | Primarily national |

| | |
|---|---|
| POSITIONING/BRANDING | |
| Customers/users are targets of sales efforts- they contribute directly to revenues "The more your sell. the more money you make." | Often users of service cannot/ do not contribute all revenues- "The more you sell, the more you may lose." |
| Differentiation through branding, packaging- benefits direct, tangible | Harder to differentiate services and demonstrate effects |
| Easy ways to demonstrate and promote Unique Selling Proposition | Benefits often long term, not readily apparent, may even be "negative" |
| OPERATIONS/DELIVERY | |
| Well trained specialists motivated by profit . | Paid and volunteer staffs, boards motivated by social goals |

# Be Wary Of "Life Cycle" Thinking!

One "fact of life" we've heard from nonprofits that experience a stage of no growth is that it must be caused by the inevitable life cycle of business and now they are destined to be in a period of decline. The feeling is that there is nothing they could do about it. For readers not aware of the life cycle theory perhaps some explanation is necessary.

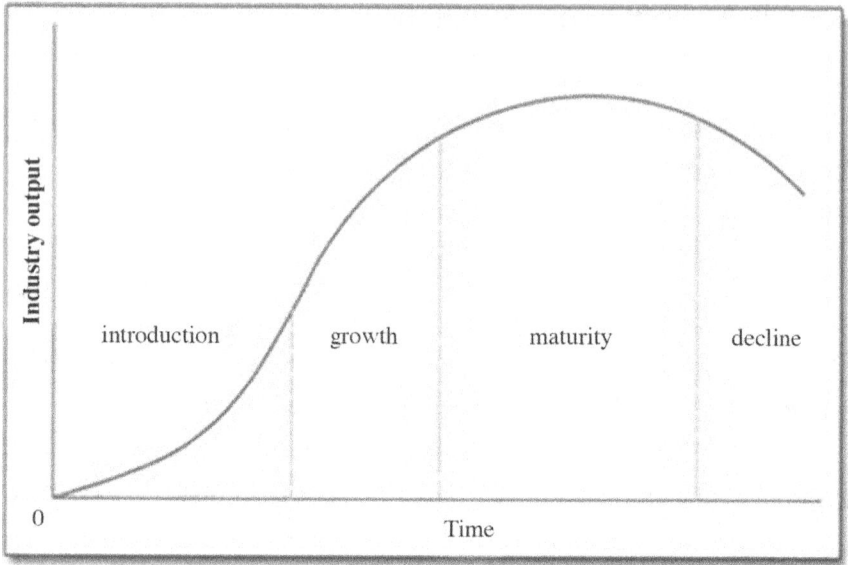

The model above was created to explain the evolution of a product and the various stages that it might go through. At each stage a different marketing response was suggested and it has been applied to business cycles as well. It is popular because intuitively it makes sense in patterning itself after the human life cycle. We are born, grow, mature and go into decline.

At best, this model is oversimplified. There is no evidence that this biological model necessarily applies to <u>brands</u> of products or services as some have continued to flourish for years. Nor does it apply to ideas, concepts or businesses. At worst it is dangerous because it becomes a <u>self-fulfilling prophecy</u>. If you think that you have reached maturity and are ready for decline, you usually act in a way that speeds up this decline.

What the model does not show is the various options you have to ensure your nonprofit never going into decline. One option, particularly if you have strong brand equity, is to reposition (See Chapter 8). For example, the March of Dimes, in its early years, was associated with mothers, infants, polio, and President Roosevelt who suffered from infantile paralysis. (If you'll look at the dime in your pocket you'll find that Roosevelt profile.) When polio became less of a threat, the March of Dimes still used its brand equity with mothers and infants and successfully repositioned to focus on birth defects, premature birth and infant mortality.

Other options include finding a new niche, or another alliance or partner, or even to create a new Power Circle. A powerful and distinctive brand may never die.

So be wary of Life Cycle thinking and forget about stages. Actually a nonprofit is a fluid, continually evolving creation. The challenge to the Leader and the Power Circle is to aid in that evolution.

# EXERCISE:

How much of the Good news-Bad news "findings" apply to your nonprofit?

What's your view of the life cycle?

Do you agree with the fundamental differences between for profits and nonprofits?

# CHAPTER 2

# WHAT DO WE MEAN BY STREET SMARTS? DIFFERENCES BETWEEN LEADERS AND MANAGERS

**"Being Street smart is not a gene or a specific talent. It is an attitude - - consisting of a vision that others don't have - - and the guts to do something to accomplish that vision."**
**Catherine Lenihan**

There are lots of words or phrases that describe people with street smarts. Some are: practical, savvy; non-Ivory tower; graduates of the school of hard knocks, in-the-trench thinkers; they know the lessons that a business school won't teach, etc.

The dictionary defines street smarts as a combination of practical skills and attitude to survive and thrive in difficult or dangerous situations. (See Street Wise) Street Smart Leaders seem to defy conventional wisdom (it's too conventional and not particularly wise). As we stated before:

- They realize that even nonprofits have to be "profitable" i.e. mutually beneficial to all parties concerned;
- They grow from the inside out rather than the outside in - growth is organic;
- They plan from the bottom up and market and promote from the top down
- They <u>focus</u> on relatively few people (we call them the Vital Few) who form a Power Circle – and who "buy" totally into the Vision of the Leader and the unique benefit provided by the nonprofit.
- They are <u>Great Listeners</u> and not necessarily only Talkers. When they do tell stories about their nonprofits it is less about WHAT they do and more about WHY they do it. Other people then share in telling these stories.
- They understand that in most cases they will have limited size and resources but these make them more flexible and able to respond faster to competition. They realize that their most important job is Chief Hurdle Removing Officer!
- And they realize that Street Smart Leadership does not reside in any one person. It is a shared and collective process, particularly of beliefs, that is spread through a select network of people – donors, clients, volunteers, boards, and staff.

The question is not how smart are you? – But HOW are you smart? Howard Gardner who wrote the <u>Theory of Multiple Intelligences</u> in 1983, suggested that we each have different ways of being intelligent. The conventional IQ predicts how well you might do on school subjects but really doesn't predict success in business, politics, the arts or nonprofits.

Warren Buffett who is one of the most Street Smart people around says: "I don't have to be smart about everything. I didn't deliver my wife's baby. So I believe in using people who are smarter than I am."

There are other supplementary skills and attributes:

- Experience from life, usually not taught from text books or schools, particularly focusing on what's working - - people, programs, processes -- rather than dwelling on what's not.
- View that most problems are really opportunities; they are "careful" risk takers and are quick to track results.
- Coaching abilities - starting with beliefs and moving to skills.
- Good "Chunkers" – they divide noble goals and missions into achievable reasonable objectives that the Vital Few can see and celebrate.
- Lastly they are persistent in stating their beliefs and getting others to buy into them. As Einstein said: "It's not that I'm so smart; it's that I stay with it".

Being Street Smart is first a way of thinking and second, a way of doing – responding to challenges and opportunities. . As a way of thinking, we've found that they tend to be LEADERS rather than just MANAGERS. This distinction becomes even more important as we rely on technology to manage mundane tasks.

In John P. Kotter's book, Leading Change, he notes that 80% of executives are preoccupied with being managers. They try to make a complicated system work through planning, staffing, etc. BUT only 20% act as leaders – sharing beliefs for a company's existence and creating and adapting organizations to constantly changing circumstances. He suggests that most of the problems in the United States come from a preoccupation with management activities rather than leadership.

Some vital differences between Leaders and Managers:

- Leaders feel that people are key, emphasize relation- ships and help others to succeed; Leaders stress <u>why</u> we are in business. Managers feel that systems, proce- dures are key and use guidelines and rules to help the organization. Managers stress <u>what we do</u>.
- Leaders promote effectiveness- their job is to inspire, coach and develop; Managers promote efficiency – their job is to direct and keep down costs.
- Leaders are aware of technology's limitations and blend high "touch" with high "tech"; Managers tend to use technology to substitute for people.

In his typical fashion, Peter Drucker says that "ninety percent of what we call management consists of making it difficult for people to get things done."

Kotter was talking primarily about large US corporations but the distinction between managing and leading is just as appropri- ate for nonprofits. Many have reached a "twilight" or "maturity" zone of non-growth brought about by being content with a cer- tain size of organization and the status quo. To this complacency, add the complexities of shared power, multiple bottom lines and managerial/board conflict over the need for change.

By Leaders we are not suggesting the stereotypic "Lone Ranger", who runs the organization by dint of his/her charisma or personality. These extroverts like to be centers of attention and may feel threatened by others who take too much initia- tive. In fact, in non-profits self-confident executives can be risky. Street Smart leaders understand the special culture of a non- profit and how important shared beliefs are to its very existence.

As Lao-Tzu observed, "A leader is best when people barely know he exists, when his work is done, his aim fulfilled, they will say: we did it ourselves".

# CASE 1

# SMILE TRAIN - - A STREET SMART NONPROFIT THAT BLENDS THE BEST OF BUSINESS THINKING WITH SOCIAL SERVICE

Smile Train was founded in 1999 and chartered in New York. Its primary mission was to provide free corrective surgery for children with cleft lip and palate in the US and developing countries (particularly in China and India). By 2011, Smile Train had assisted some 650,000 children in 74 countries and raised $91 million in 2009.

## A HIGHLY MOTIVATED ""POWER CIRCLE"

Smile Train started with a strong sense of passion of its founder, Brian Mullaney, and blended with his mantra of a "charity that is run like a business." He had considerable experience working with cosmetic surgeons, advertising agencies and with Operation Smile, another nonprofit that also performed free corrective surgery. He attracted Charles Wang as a partner who paired his philanthropic interest with his technological expertise to provide state of the art operations. The Executive Director, Priscilla Ma, has provided continuity of overall supervision through dynamic growth and with such leaders as Mullaney and Wang the Board boasts VIP Directors such as Stephen Colbert, Colin Powell, Hillary Swan, and the late Walter Cronkite.

## UNIQUE POSITIONING AND BRAND STRATEGY – THAT TOLD SMILE TRAIN'S STORY. - - WHY THEY WERE IN BUSINESS.

- For users, patients and families. - - The corrective surgery not only resolved a physical problem but more importantly helped remove the social ostracism and psychological scarring that accompanied disfigurement. (Some babies were actually smothered by midwives in certain countries.)
- For donors –This powerful emotional appeal carried over to donors. The "before and after" pictures demonstrated dramatic change not only esthetically but culturally. Operations were translated into equivalent donations - - and donors could see immediate results of their donations.The story was told in word and pictures.

The promotional program throughout used the logo (a smiling train) the brand name, Smile Train, plus positioning tag line "Changing the World One Smile a Time." This was a very user friendly approach since the patients in the surgery were relatively young and could be frightened of surgeons and hospitals.

## SUPERIOR VALUE DELIVERY SYSTEM

This was probably the key to success. Unlike competitive programs which featured sending American medical professionals to target countries, Smile Train used local medical clinics, trained local professionals and charged nonwestern prices. Smile Train set up strategic alliances with hospitals which enhanced relations via peer-to-peer partnerships. This offered great advantages of speed, convenience and substantial cost-savings.

In addition Wang introduced technology and software programs to train local professionals and monitor results of operations in the various countries.

TARGETED FUND RAISING –Relationship Building and using cutting edge online and offline appeals. With a relatively small staff Smile Train was able to track and test results of various appeals, letters, and photos. They could measure results from various zip codes and even which alphabetical name would be most generous.

Donations were matched with costs of surgeries so individual donor could see what he was achieving. Heavier donors were encouraged to increase donations through matched gifts as well as joining the Smile of the Month Club (monthly pledges automatically charged to credit cards) and the Premier Circle.

The New York Times calls Smile Train one of the most productive charities – dollar for deed – in the world.

# EXERCISE:

Do you agree with some of the differences suggested between Leaders and Managers? Are you a Leader or Manager?

What lessons could you learn from the Smile Train case that might apply to your nonprofit?

How Street Smart are you? Which skills do you have that suggest you are?

# PART II: TEN SUCCESS "SECRETS" FROM STREET SMART LEADERS

# CHAPTER 3

# THEY REALIZE THAT NONPROFITS HAVE TO BE "PROFITABLE". THEY HAVE TO MAXIMIZE REVENUES AND RETURNS FOR MUTUAL BENEFITS.

**"Love your passion, but know your business."**
**Anonymous**

One word that I've never heard from Street Smart Leaders is the word <u>charity</u>. That suggests being dependent on the kindness of strangers for survival. Too often a charitable organization may feel that it is owed support because it is "doing good for people". "People ought to be listening to our information because of the urgent problems that we're trying to solve. We have a "monopoly on goodness."

For many Street Smart Leaders dividing an organization into for-profit and nonprofit is a distinction which satisfies the

Internal Revenue Service but isn't really accurate for three reasons:

1. Nonprofits are taking on for-profit subsidiaries or extensions. Many churches, museums, music and arts organizations depend on their profit arms to help supplement their nonprofit operations. For profits have established nonprofit institutes to support their philanthropic endeavors or to provide voices in the political arena.

2. The three traditional sectors, government, private enterprise and nonprofit, are overlapping and impacting each other. Almost all have set up mutual partnerships. Disasters such as the aftermath of Hurricane Katrina demonstrate how all three sectors cooperated with one another.

3. The third and most important reason is that all organizations must be "profitable" to survive, grow and become sustainable. The dictionary defines "profitability" as yielding advantageous returns, results, or benefits. For-profits use return to stakeholders as their success criterion; nonprofits use benefits to stakeholders. But these goals are on a continuum and not an "either/or" situation.

In a speech given to TED in March, 2013, Dan Pallotta, activist and fund raiser, decries the double standard that seems to operate when it comes to expectations for profits and nonprofits.

"They seem to operate under two different rulebooks. For example, there seems to be a visceral reaction to the notion that anyone should make very much money helping people. If you want to make $50 million selling violent video games to kids, we'll put you on the cover of Wired Magazine, but if you want to make $50 million trying to cure malaria, you're considered a parasite yourself. For-profit companies can spend as much as they want on promotion but for some reason such expenditures are unseemly for nonprofits. The same thing seems to apply to overhead since there will be less available for the "cause." In a strange way nonprofits are rewarded for how little they spend on salaries, promotion and overhead rather than on their accomplishments. We tend to equate frugality with morality."

The leader of any modern nonprofit has dual objectives; to advance social/public welfare AND the survival and growth of the enterprise. Concentrating only on a service orientation without using good business principles can be a weakness and not strength.

## TIPS FROM STREET SMART LEADERS:

1. Listen to Peter Drucker, the guru of nonprofits, and talk about customers (these are all of our stakeholders) and try to develop their loyalty since they are more profitable (cost effective). We ought to think about the "life time value" of a loyal donor or user.

2. The operative word is BENEFITS for all concerned: donors, staffs, boards, and volunteers. And these benefits must be mutual. It is not only what donors can give to the nonprofit, but what they get out of their contribution. The same applies to volunteers and board members.

3. The more you can quantify and measure these benefits the better the organization will be. Get into the habit of testing, measuring and optimizing. Figure out what's working and do more of it.

4. Learn the advantages of using the new media to supplement your one-on-one relationships with shareholders, i.e. donors, volunteers, staffs, boards, media, etc.

5. As your boards are increasingly made up of retired or active business persons you'll have to feel more comfortable with some of the jargon of business — co-branding, market share, and promotional mixes, etc.

6. MOST IMPORTANTLY FOR SMALL NONPROFITS. Your best growth strategy is from the inside out rather than the outside in.

   As Tom Peters reminds us: The ROI (return on investments) that truly matters is ROIR (return on investment in <u>relationships</u>.) Success is all about developing AND keeping good relationships.

7. To find oil you have to dig wells. Try it out - - look for things that are going right and build on them. Some of the best nonprofits have experimented their way to success.

## EXERCISE:

Imagine that your nonprofit is having its annual meeting a year from now. At this meeting you would be celebrating your greatest achievements from the previous year. How many involve money as a criterion? (ROI) What about ROIR (return on investment in relationships)?

I often ask the key decision makers of a nonprofit that if I could give them $10,000 right now and they could put it into a <u>single</u> activity, person or event that would have the most impact, where would they put it?

Usually there is a good deal of hemming and hawing for a while and several suggestions reveal a pet project or prejudice. BUT, after a period, some consensus will be reached and produce a very neatly targeted suggestion. This should be the point of focus and leveraging for next year. What would you do with that $10,000?

## CASE 2

## THE TOMS SHOE COMPANY: A TREND FOR THE FUTURE? A FOR-PROFIT OPERATING A NONPROFIT?

TOMS shoes is a for-profit company based in Santa Monica, California that also operates a non-profit subsidiary called Friends of TOMS.

The driving force behind the company and the subsidiary is Blake Mycoskie an entrepreneur from Arlington, Texas. While competing on the second season of the Amazing race he visited Argentina. There he noted Argentine farmers wearing ALPARGATA shoes, a type of espadrille.

He decided to open a business in US to sell this type of shoe but with added wrinkle that for every pair of TOMS purchased a pair of new shoes would be given to a child in need. As of this date over 1,000,000 pairs have been given in 20 countries worldwide, including US as well as Argentina, Ethiopia, Rwanda, Guatemala, Haiti and South Africa.

Mycoskie emphasizes his company's goal is not only to give shoes but to also educate others on importance of wearing shoes. Children without shoes in these countries are susceptible to health risks and may not be allowed to go to school.

With help from other nonprofit organizations and non-governmental organizations TOMS is able to give shoes to children in need year-round. Friends of TOMS coordinate "shoe drops" around the world for employees and volunteers to experience TOM"S giving first hand. On June 7, 2011, TOMS launched a new product user the One to One Model, sunglasses and it is associated with TOMS' giving partner, SEVA foundation.

## NOTES:

_____

_____

_____

_____

_____

_____

_____

_____

_____

_____

_____

_____

_____

# CHAPTER 4

# THEY FOLLOW THE 80/20 RULE-THEY FOCUS ON THE 20% -PEOPLE, PROGRAMS AND RESOURCES –THAT PRODUCE 80% OF THE RESULTS.

**"There is an art of clearing away the clutter and focusing on what matters most. It is simple and transferable. It just requires the courage to take a different approach."**
**George Anders**

The legend is that the 80/20 rule had its origins in a garden that grew pea pods! This garden was special and was owned by Vilfredo Pareto, an Italian economist and part-time gardener. He observed that most of his pea pods were coming from relatively few of his pea plants! Perhaps that incident triggered some his later research when in the late 1890s he published the Pareto Principle based on observations of 19th century England that showed that most income and wealth went to a minority of people

Building on Pareto's principle, George K. Zipf, introduced the "Principle of Least Effort" which found that productive resources tended to arrange themselves to minimize work. He was the first to start using ratios to express this difference- - 20 -30% - - accounting for 70-80% of the results.

In 1951 Joseph Moses Juran applied the Pareto Principle to quality control issues. He suggested that 20% of the tasks are responsible for 80% of the results. (The "Vital Few" and the "Trivial Many.")

(For a good review of these principles and specific sources, the best book is The 80/20 Principle by Richard Koch, Doubleday Publishers, 1998. It can be found with other helpful sources in the Desert Island Book list in the Appendix.)

No matter what its name may be - - I prefer the 80/20 Rule - - it states that there is an inbuilt imbalance between causes and results, inputs and outputs, effort and reward. A minority of inputs leads to a majority of outputs. When this imbalance is measured quantitatively, it usually winds up in a surprisingly high relationship or ratio of 80/20 - - 80% of results may come from only 20% of our inputs. This imbalance is systematic and predictable.

Koch points out that why this principle is so important is that it is so counterintuitive. We seem to expect that 50% of causes will account for 50% of results or outputs. There seems to be a natural almost democratic expectation that causes and outputs will come out balanced. But they don't.

For profit companies have used these rules of thumb for years:

- 80% of their profits come from 20% of their customers (so do 80% of their complaints). 80% of their sales come from 20% of their products or services.
- 80% of their sales are made by 20% of their sales staff.
- 80% of your most innovative ideas come from 20% of your employees.

In Healthcare, 20% of patients use 80% of health care resources. In the financial service industry, 20% of customers generate positive income while 80% cost the company money. Microsoft knows that fixing 20% of the most reported bugs would eliminate 80% of errors and crashes.

(Even in your personal lives, you'll find that you wear 20% of your wardrobe 80% of the time. And probably 80% of your arguments with spouse or partner are caused by 20% of the topics about which you disagree - - for most couples it's money, who does domestic chores and child-raising.)

Street Smart Leaders convert this rule into action. They focus most of their attention on the Vital Few - - people, programs, processes - - the 20% -- that produce most of the results –the 80%. In their planning they realize that although there may be multiple goals or objectives or missions, a critical few are more important than all of the others combined.

In essence, they become 80/20 thinkers – using the 80/20 formula to solve problems and take advantage of opportunities. It is an integral part of their strategic planning, implementing and decision-making.

How then, in our nonprofit world, do we start becoming 80/20 Thinkers (or more accurately rethinkers?) and Doers?

# SOME TIPS FROM STREET SMART LEADERS

1. FOCUS on the VITAL FEW- - high impact people, programs, and operations --that are working and stop doing the ones that aren't. Concentrate on the 20% that produce 80% of your results. If you're not sure of what's working or not, go out in the field and REALLY LISTEN to your stakeholders. - -They'll be quick to tell you.

   On a personal note, I've found that focusing may actually expand a service. While working with hospitals that specialized in an operation for weight loss, we discovered that patients losing weight was only the first step. The hospital had to provide services to make sure that this change would be permanent. Examples;

   - Provide support groups for those who had gone through the procedure;
   - Create online advice about diets, physical activities at home
   - Create physical exercise facilities at the hospital or guest passes at other convenient spas
   - Educate as to clothing, cosmetics, to reinforce self-image.

   Sometimes it is just a shift in focus. For example, one hospital had problems with nurse turnover. We investigated why nurses were staying not why they were leaving. This helped find out what was working, and not what wasn't.

2. LEVERAGE – whatever energies, people, and money you have to support what's working - - just do more of it and better. You really don't need more money or people - you really have sufficient resources - but they have to be realigned using the 80/20 rule. This rule helps you find the

DISCONNECTS between what you DO and what you ACHIEVE.

3.  MEASURE AND TRACK RESULTS - - to see if 1 and 2 are producing - -if they are not, be quick to make changes and start the cycle again.

4.  TAKE ADVANTAGE OF BEING SMALL—

    *   Small can mean flexibility - -you can react faster to changes and respond more quickly to competition;
    *   Small can mean keeping things simple and eliminating layers of bureaucracy. The reasons that many large for profit companies don't use 80/20 rule effectively is their middle managers seem to love complexity and to make things complicated.
    *   Small means that it's easier to spot and keep the VITAL FEW -- people, programs and processes that are working- and get rid of the TRIVIAL MANY that are not.
    *   Small means resiliency - -you can make mistakes but correct them and keep on going.

    Being small helps to get the Vital Few to buy into your belief system - - what benefits do you provide or problems that you solve – that make you truly different. The why over the what!

5.  Use 80/20 thinking in your work week. As David Thoreau said: "It's not enough to be busy...so are the ants. The question is what are we busy about?" Managers tend to equate Busyness with effectiveness; Leaders work smarter not harder.

# 80/20 THINKING SUMMARIZED...SOME IMPLICATIONS.

- Understand that 20 percent of your fundraisers, volunteers, board members, and resources will produce 80 percent of your results. THEY ARE THE TRUE BELIEVERS IN WHAT MAKES YOU DIFFERENT
- Limit your goals, objectives, programs, resources. Focus on the Vital Few.
- Plan from the bottom up, not the top down. Adapt along the way!
- Think sequentially, not concurrently. No multitasking!
- Market and promote from the inside out, not from the outside in. (Let your Power Circle do it with "elevator speeches" and telling your story.)
- Focus on what's working and don't worry about what's not. Do what you're doing—but do it better.
- Leverage the resources you already have (people, time, money, and image) instead of focusing on resources you think you have to get.
- Measure small steps, not a grand vision. Keep Chunking! Allow for safe successes, and be quick to adapt, make changes, and use benchmarks.
- Failure to grow is more a lack of will than resources or capacity. You really have all of the tools you need. It's how you use them. So experiment your way to success.
- Remember LESS IS MORE. Start using a To Don't List rather than a To Do list. What activities should you stop doing today?

# EXERCISE:

The following list contains 20 components that can con-tribute most to the success of a non-profit. Using the 80/20 framework pick out the FOUR elements that you think added the most value to your non-profit last year. Feel free to add any component not in the list.

| PEOPLE (their expertise, enthusiasm) | ✓ | MARKETING/ POSITIONING | ✓ |
|---|---|---|---|
| Management team, staff | | Promotion, marketing effectiveness | |
| Board of directors | | Public relations, community relations | |
| Volunteers, individuals, groups | | Fundraising, capital campaigns | |
| Partners, outside alliances | | Grant writing, lobbying contacts | |
| | | Referral sources | |
| | | Branding, logo, creative campaigns | |
| **MANAGEMENT EXPERTISE** | ✓ | **PROGRAMS/ FACILITIES** | ✓ |
| Program planning, meetings, | | Service program quality | |
| Budgeting, project/program control | | Service program volume, activity | |

| | | | |
|---|---|---|---|
| Technological expertise, data processing | | State of art, up-to-date facilities | |
| Internal administrative processes | | Administrative Office Technologies | |
| Good relationships among all participants | | | |
| Overall financial health | | | |

# CASE 3

## THE JITTERBUG CELL PHONE

A great example of 80/20 Thinking and Design.

Engineers and product designers keep adding more features into more innovations. It seems to be something of a contest! Modern cell phones have become smaller (making them hard to read particularly for "older' users.) They have applications which many callers really don't need and can't even operate (like playing music, taking pictures or surfing the internet.) And, of course, they all involve complicated pricing plans and long-term contracts. The focus is always on the what – what the phone can do.

Enter the Jitterbug cell phone. It has put in 20% of the features that provide 80% of the benefits for older users who simply want something like their old phones, but portable. Jitterbug has simplified everything with large backlit displays of numbers you can actually read. They have an "O" feature to contact a real human operator if you want a phone number or help in case of an accident. There is even a dial tone. They have simplified pricing and eliminated long term contracts. They focused on why this phone is necessary particularly for people who want something user-friendly. .

Most promotion was in magazines like AARP catering to the older demographic, but they've broadened their promotion to all people who desire a simpler, easier to use, and more or less familiar way to communicate.

39

## EXERCISE:

1. Introspect a bit about the 80/20 Rule. Do you agree with its basic premise? Why or why not?

2. What about your nonprofit? Have you noticed patterns? For example;
   20% of your volunteers do most of the work?

   20% of your board members seem to be the most active?

   20% of your donors contribute 80% of your donations? Any other examples?

3. How do you think you could best use 80/20 thinking in your nonprofit?

**EXERCISE:** Applying 80/20 Thinking to your work week.

"Focus is a matter of deciding the things you're NOT going to do."

John Carmack

For some reason Americans pride themselves on how many hours per week they work (they passed the Japanese last year). Taking work home is a badge of honor. One needs to be connected at all times – cell phones, texting, checking emails, etc. And there seem to be meetings, meetings, meetings. They love to multitask. Steve Uzzell says that "multitasking is merely the opportunity to screw up more than one thing at a time."

Street Smart Leaders use the 80/20 rule in organizing their work week. Apply the 80/20 rule to your work week. Which activities do you think you could eliminate - that really are not contributing to your mission/goal? Which ones should you focus on?

Did you know that most executives spend almost a third of their work week reading and answering their email? Can you cut this down? Some suggest limiting all emails to only 5 sentences – others write in advance what they say and then cut it in half. How could you use the 80/20 rule here?

# NOTES:

_____

_____

_____

_____

_____

_____

_____

_____

_____

_____

_____

_____

_____

# CHAPTER 5

# STREET SMART LEADERS DO "BOTTOM UP" PLANNING AND "TOP-DOWN" MARKETING

**Planning is bringing the future into the present
so that you can do something about it now.**
**Alan Laikin**

Let's face it! Trying to change minds is a difficult thing. What you're asking people to do is forget one set of perceptions and start remembering another - - not an easy task. Think of the countless Wars that we've engaged in: poverty, drugs, terrorists, equal rights, literacy, etc – and in many cases the situation may be worse now than before.

It's obviously a case of coming up with a powerful business plan that can work. Surprisingly few nonprofits actually have a business plan or know how the planning process works. Jim Moran's best selling One Page Business Plan with special editions for Busy Executives, Women in Business, Creative

Entrepreneurs claims sales in the thousands – not much of a dent in the 1 ½ million non profits in the US.

The largest nonprofits with their huge resources, size and clout tend to do Top-Down planning: mission, objectives, strategies, tactics and budgeting. To these nonprofits STRATEGIES DICTATE TACTICS. Many of the planners see themselves as Generals which is what the word in Greek really means: "Strategos"- what army leaders or generals do.

The few smaller nonprofits that do any business planning tend to follow the lead of the larger ones and do top-down planning. It looks something like this:

## Top Down Planning (One Size Fits All)

They spend 80% of their time and energy on defining their mission/vision, with multiple goals and objectives, multiple strategies and programs and 20% of their time on the action plans and budgets. Since they don't have annual business plans, there is a tendency to have a one-size-fits-all plan that covers everything. In most cases they assume that the workers (volunteers, staff) will buy into their ambitious goals and objectives. IN SHORT TOO MANY OVERPLAN AND UNDEREXECUTE.

But Street Smart Leaders of smaller nonprofits with their limited resources and perhaps more realistic ambitions do the OPPOSITE! They feel that A STRONG TACTIC DICTATES STRATEGIES. (Incidentally tactics is also derived from the Greek but it is what the foot soldiers do!) So the name of the game is to find a distinctive competitive angle that makes you really different.

They follow this model:

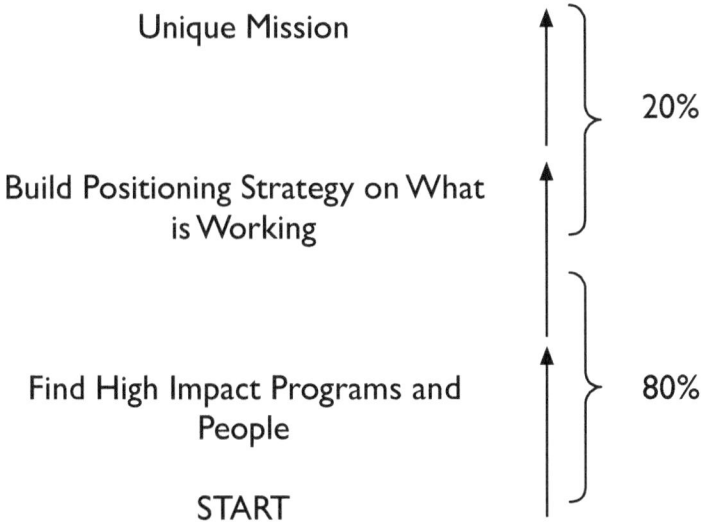

## Bottom Up Planning (Unique Difference)

Unique Mission

20%

Build Positioning Strategy on What is Working

Find High Impact Programs and People

80%

START

The tactic becomes the point of attack and the strategy is the process of organizing the operation to give maximum thrust to that unique competitive angle. The key is to be the first to exploit this tactic, to fortify and support it, and to pre-empt others from imitating. Remember Positioning rewards the first one who is in the customer's or donor's mind.

Focusing on a powerful tactic and building on this for a single strategy – a coherent direction –is easier to sell to the Power Circle since they are not distracted by conflicting directions.

In the Annual Bishop's Fund case (see Chapter 12) we went out into the parishes to find the competitive angle that was really working and meant most to parishioners. It was that the proceeds and collections from the fund came back to the local priests so that they could work on their unique local problems. Parishioners could see neighbors who were being helped. The tactic was built into a strategy "Support the Bishop's Fund be-cause it supports you."

Of course going out into the streets to find out what really makes you different may come up with some surprises. You may find out that what you thought was your key difference was really not. Or worse yet you may find that you don't have an important perceived difference. This in itself would be a critical insight and would put more emphasis on finding "that difference that makes a difference".

If you're a new nonprofit the last thing you want to project is what you think the key differences might be or make up tac-tics to support some grand strategy. It's crucial to get out into the streets to find out what that critical niche might be.

In sum, get your Power Circle members mobilized to see what programs and people are working and REALLY LISTEN TO what customers think you do best. Then build these into

positioning strategies ("Oh – they're the people who _____")
and their elevator speeches (benefit and supporting features.)

Leverage your resources on the VITAL FEW programs or
people that are working. Strategy comes from high impact tactics and programs that make a difference and not the other
way around.

Street Smart Leaders find out what they're good at and
build their entire organization around that knowledge.

In understanding the difference between Grand Strategies
and Critical tactics we can take a lesson from professional golf-
ers. Their favorite expression is that You Drive for Show (the
great strategy) but that You Putt for Dough (that powerful
tactic!)

---

The second important difference between the Mega
Nonprofits and the smaller nonprofits is that the "Biggies" like
to think of themselves as generals and thus relegate or del-
egate marketing to the field troops. Smaller nonprofits realize
that effective marketing must come from the top down.

Whenever I've worked with smaller nonprofits I often run into a lot of misconceptions about marketing.

## MARKETING 101 - - SHORT COURSE

Marketing is everything you do to grow your nonprofit. All of your stakeholders – volunteers, staff, boards and donors – are actually marketers! Your pattern of growth should always be from the inside out, which may preclude spending great sums on external advertising or promotion. In most cases with limited resources you probably can't afford them anyway.

Marketing is a mind-set AND a set of activities. Too many people focus on the activities – pricing, delivering, promoting – and not enough think about the mind-set. This challenges you to think about your service from the point of view of the user and not the seller.

Many nonprofits don't really know what business they are in. They focus so much on the operations side. There is a great difference between what you're selling and what people are really buying.

Ted Levitt reminds us that the hardware customer does not want to buy a half-inch drill - - he wants a half-inch hole. Funeral directors don't sell caskets, people buy peace of mind. Consultants don't sell market research; the client wants to solve a problem. Florists may sell flowers but the customers are really buying thoughtfulness. Orthodontists don't sell braces; people are really buying middle-class respectability.

Many businessmen tend to equate marketing with promotion, it really is much more. It has to do with building and maintaining relationships, looking for "moments of truth" when a service fails and you have to fix it, and internal marketing since often your service is really a person.

One of the most important ingredients of marketing is selling. Yes, selling…and this is where the negative comments usually start coming in. Unfortunately because of the negative stereotypes of salespeople, critics tend to judge them at their worst (aluminum siding, used cars, telemarketers, etc.) rather than at their best (a Sam Walton, Bill Gates, or a Thomas Watson). Watson was the man who built IBM and his mantra was "Nothing happens until someone sells something." That "something" could be a product or service but it can be an idea or concept, a political party or a country. Clergymen, politicians and professors may not like the word but they are constantly "selling".

Because of its reputation, professionals have other words for salespeople. They are called "rainmakers" in law firms and usually make senior partners. Others are account executives or client developers, or outreach specialists - - but they <u>are</u> sales people. In fact almost all of the organizations I've worked with consist of three groups: GRINDERS – they do basic day-to-day work; MINDERS – who supervise the grinders; and the FINDERS –the Rainmakers who make the organization grow.

And that's where your Power Circle comes in - - they are your Finders! They are your Vital Few armed with their Elevator Speeches, select list of clients, and their promotional packages. (See related chapters on Elevator Speeches, donor strategies, and promotion.) Remember not everyone can sell - - there's that 80/20 rule again - - 20% of your people will make 80% of your sales .They will have individual styles and approaches but one thing they can do is close make an offer and get an acceptance.

I'm often surprised how nonprofits dislike selling themselves or persuading others to accept their ideas or services. Persuading is nothing new. Way back in the Third Century BC, Aristotle suggested the three elements of persuasion:

ETHOS – your character – what you stand for.

PATHOS – what feeling do you invoke – most importantly trust.

LOGOS – logic – how you help person justify, rationalize the decision.

Not a bad formula for persuading or selling your nonprofit.

# TIPS FROM STREET SMART LEADERS ON PLANNING

1.  Most mission statements sound like Boy Scout oaths - -re-flecting good intentions. Your mission statement should contain three ingredients: <u>who</u> do we serve-to what end and why; what issue/needs/problem do we work on; how do we solve that problem?

2.  Because of the infrequency of planning and the "shared power" issues over turf/territory, goals/missions, resources, most nonprofits spend too much time, (80%), on top down components and not enough time and energy (20%) on action plans. Planners often underestimate the time and complexity of their plans and fail to factor in other considerations, such as money, people and time. In short, too much time is devoted to PLANNING THE WORK AND NOT ENOUGH ON WORKING THE PLAN.

3.  Most business plans look like shopping lists with little thought of sequencing and cause and effect. (What has to be done first before anything else can happen?) Too often internal necessities like recruiting, staffing and training are confused with external objectives like increasing funds, getting more members. (See the XYZ Jazz Federation and Metropolitan Small Business Cases.)

4.  Actually the key is learning the planning <u>process</u> not necessarily the <u>plan</u>. Tom Peters, in his usual nonconventional style, says that once you have the plan and everybody has read and understood it, then you BURN IT. Too often the Business Plan becomes an all-powerful document that cannot be changed or altered even though we know that <u>half of the business plans will not succeed in the first year</u>.

5. The world is changing fast; our ability to understand is slow. So don't wait for the one-size-fits-all plan. Start Testing; make an offer- a low risk one —and see what happens. Success is built <u>sequentially</u>, one thing at a time – one service, one program, one experience. Planning is from the bottom up —tactic to strategy.

6. For each high impact program, the process is started over again - - as often as necessary. That's why learning the Business Planning PROCESS is essential - -not just the Plan. <u>Street Smart leaders experiment their way to success</u>.

7. Your Power Circle members act as champions for a particular program and should know the Planning Process backwards and forwards. The more they participate in the process the more it becomes THEIR plan and not the organization's plan.

8. Just expecting people to buy into the plan is not enough. You will have to MODEL what you value and VALUE what you model. Increasingly people care less about what you say and MORE about what you do.

**You can't change people. You must be the change you wish in people.**
**Gandhi**

## MODELING WHAT YOU VALUE

I was surprised to find that many board members of symphony orchestras, art museums and opera companies didn't have season tickets for their nonprofit institution. . If they didn't value the creative output of their nonprofit and believe that attendance was truly worthwhile why should others? Street Smart LEADERS not only share the BELIEFS that they think are important BUT they model what those behaviors should be. Tom Peters suggests that Leaders be very tight on their values but looser in how people might accomplish their actions. He touts Managing by Walking Around.

I found out about this need to model the hard way when I was Director of the Executive MBA Program at Tulane. Throughout I stressed to my staff how important it was to be around on the weekends because that's when Murphy's Law kicked in. (e.g. projectors were not available, the caterers and the food would be late, or there would be parking problems.) As a tenured full professor I "naturally" exempted myself from this rule.

One Saturday I had an appointment on campus and stopped by to see how the EMBA program was doing and found that practically no one from the staff was around. Later when I pointed out this problem, the explanation I received was that if I really believed in how important it was for everyone to be around on weekends I would have been there. Obviously there was a DISCONNECT. Suffice it to say, I was around every Saturday morning from then on.

## REWARDING WHAT YOU VALUE

I have been fortunate to be on the faculty of three excellent universities: Minnesota, Texas (at Austin) - -two state nonprofit organizations –and Tulane University – a private nonprofit.

Whenever one of these institutions appointed a new president we on the faculty always expected the announcement of a new "strategic plan". This usually came about through consultations with Deans, Regents and powerful alumni but rarely with the faculty. The president might set up faculty meetings to announce the plan but it was more for purposes of information than feedback. If there were suggestions from the faculty they were usually "too late" because one didn't want to disrupt the plan.

As a result the faculty perceived the plan to be the President's plan not 'ours". With almost a feeling of relief we could go back to our teaching and research. Not surprisingly not much ever did change because the faculty did not "buy into the plan." They saw no incentives or rewards to implement the plan. Perhaps that's why over half of most business plans don't make it through the first year.

# SOME TIPS ABOUT MARKETING AND SELLING

1. Everybody does marketing! One of the worst things a small nonprofit can do is hire someone either internally or externally to do marketing. Once you do that everyone else abdicates his/her role of growing your nonprofit. They will depend on this one person to do all of the contact work. Marketing is too important to be left to a single person. Your Heavy Donors, most active volunteers and board members, your staff must take on that responsibility.

2. Since you will grow from the inside out, INTERNAL marketing is more important than EXTERNAL marketing. You have to get everybody on the same page and the Leader has to model expectations. You can't talk about how important marketing is if you can't do it yourself.

3. Since everybody does marketing you should observe who has most contact in your nonprofit with users and donors and make sure that they consider themselves marketers. That's particularly important for staff who answer the phone or volunteers who represent your nonprofit. Look at Disney and see how they train everybody who has contact with guests to help and advise them. Even executives have to come back each year to work in a Disney Park to see what happens at the contact level.

4. A forgotten market for nonprofits is the people who make referrals. They can be physicians or social workers or other professionals who recommend your nonprofit. The 80/20 rule works here and 20% of your referrers will do 80% of the referrals. They also want to be recognized and thanked for their business. Too often they are taken for granted - - NEVER DO THIS!

5.  Most services, for profit and nonprofit, tend to overprom-
    ise and under deliver. This builds up unreasonable expecta-
    tions and most can't back up these promises. It is better to
    under promise and over deliver.

6.  I've never understood why sales people have such bad rep-
    utations. Perhaps people say this because they themselves
    can't sell. Selling is a talent like everything else. Relatively
    few people can really sell - - and I mean make an offer and
    get an acceptance. There are lots of people that the pro-
    fession calls schmoozers – they are sociable, glad-handers
    but they really can't sell. That's why that 80/20 rule applies.
    20% of your sales people will do 80% of your sales. So you
    want to make sure when you recruit your Power Circle
    that they can sell.

7.  I've been told that you can't turn a non sales person into
    a sales person and you cannot keep a salesperson from
    selling. If that's true I really don't have much time to try to
    train them.

# CASE 4 – XYZ JAZZ FEDERATION

Most nonprofit plans have <u>too many goals</u> and objectives and bundle <u>supply</u> side objectives; dealing with operations and costs, with <u>demand</u> side; marketing and fundraising. The lack of focus may lead to frustration and a feeling that the plan is not working.

The following are objectives for the nonprofit:

1. Set up 10 music educational programs in local high schools and colleges.

2. Provide musical scholarships to 10 minority students annually.

3. Increase grants from the state-wide Arts Foundation from $100,000 to $300,000.

4. Create five jazz awards and announce at annual gala awards ceremony.

5. Increase staff from five to eight.

6. Increase volunteers from thirty to sixty.

7. Increase performance revenue from $120K to $250K.

8. Increase membership from 300 to 500 and revenue from $400K to $500K.

9. Launch capital campaign and hire consultant and grant writer.

Six of these objectives focus on the supply or operations side and involve significant costs and expenses. (1,2,4,5,,6,9) and three focus on the demand side (3, 6, and 7) and entail considerable implementation costs.

When we apply the 80/20 Rule, only Objectives 7 and 8 MIGHT HAVE SUFFICIENT PAYOFF FOR FOCUS AND LEVERAGE.

# CASE 5: METROPOLITAN SMALL BUSINESS AND ENTREPRENEURIAL ASSOCIATION

1. Recruit 20 low-income members and increase minority members by 10%.

2. Set up three joint ventures with local colleges and their small business institutes and conduct six workshops. Generate $30,000.

3. Sponsor annual Super Bowl competition for students from 7 MBA programs who will work on and present management solutions for small businesses. Generate $50,000 from local sponsors (banks, investment houses.)

4. Award four scholarships and internships to high school and college students to attend workshops and Super Bowl. Costs $20,000.

5. Increase overall membership from 120 to 300 by end of year. Net increase of income - $180,000.

6. Recognize 5 outstanding entrepreneurs for outstanding service at awards dinner at Super Bowl.

7. Get three grants from SBA and State Development Boards for three-year commitments $300,000.

8. Send three officers to National Meetings of Entrepreneurs to learn about Management techniques. Costs $10,000.

We see <u>too many objectives</u> and very little concentra-
tion on the <u>Vital Few</u>. The next question is who will do all
of these ambitious projects?

For example:

Objectives 1,4, 6 and 8 - -certainly desirable from a
public relations or operations point of view are essentially
Cost Centers and not income generators. At best they can
be delayed.

Objective 3 would ultimately generate national recognition but it would require a longer time commitment -
-perhaps as much as three years to take program from test
to fulfillment.

Objective 7 certainly is worthwhile but it would require
special staffing, contacts with grant givers, and again time.

Only Objective 2 and 5 would seem to be promising
in that this nonprofit has sufficient people and resources
to generate the funds needed to support the other six
objectives.

# EXERCISE:

Bottom up Planning

Using the model in the chapter, what is your high impact program that makes up your unique critical advantage? Can you convert this into a unique positioning strategy?

The Five Universal Questions:

Whether you plan down or up, you must always ask these five basic questions:

1. WHERE ARE YOU NOW? (What's your most important strength?)

2. WHERE DO YOU WANT TO BE? (specific measurable objective)

3. HOW WILL YOU GET THERE? (Your positioning strategy? You support for that position.)

4. WHO WILL DO WHAT? WHEN? FOR HOW MUCH?

5. HOW WILL YOU KNOW YOU'RE SUCCEEDING? (What will you change if you're not?)
How would you answer these questions?

# EXERCISE:

Marketing and Selling

This chapter suggests two "off the wall" ideas: you should plan from the bottom up and market from the top down. How do you feel about these concepts? How can you use them in your nonprofit?

Do you agree with the statements that marketing is everything that your nonprofit does to grow and that everybody does marketing? How well do you model your views?

What about selling? Do you agree with Thomas Watson that "nothing happens until someone sells something? "How good of a salesperson are you?

# CHAPTER 6

# THEY FIND THEIR UNIQUE NICHE AND STICK TO IT. THEY FOCUS ON THEIR STRENGTHS - WHAT THEY DO WELL –AND DO IT BETTER. THEY ARE GREAT LISTENERS!

**Too many people going into nonprofits and philanthropy think they have all the answers. If you really want to help someone, shut up and LISTEN!**

**Ernest Sirolli, International Activist**

Street Smart Leaders early on understand FOUR basic concepts:

1. Their nonprofit cannot be everything to everybody. This runs contrary to many nonprofits that want to reach all of the public with their message. Actually there is no single public but different groups of people with different interests and motivations.

2. Niching is based on the FOCUS PARADOX- -the more you narrow your focus the more you widen your impact. When you focus you magnify. (See more of this in Positioning.)

By finding a niche, the nonprofit gets to know its stakeholders better. The Power Circle has more access to limited numbers of decision makers and it is easier to position and find the difference that makes a difference (that unique Elevator Speech).

Niching is particularly important to nonprofits with limited resources. They can emphasize a particular geographic area. Thomas P. "Tip" O'Neil said that "all politics is local". And so is the business of most nonprofits!

Niching makes it easier to come up with an elevator speech since you can focus on the most important problem you can solve for your user group OR you can focus on your most important benefit. The key here is not to let the big competitors run your nonprofit. The more you look like one of the larger nonprofits the more the stakeholders get confused and actually attribute your activities to the Big One. (See the case of the disappointed board.)

3. The best niche is the one that plays to your nonprofit's strengths - - what you do best - - and to make it even better. There isn't sufficient time or money to remedy weaknesses. One realist suggested that if you spend a great deal of time working on your weaknesses, you'll end up with lots of strong weaknesses.

4. To find those strengths you'll have to  listen!. Street Smart Leaders know the profound difference between merely hearing what people say and REALLY listening. Research on doctors indicates that rather than listening to patients describing their problems, the average doctor interrupts the patient within the first 18 seconds. Tom Peters says that this is  true of most managers and calls them 18 second managers. (As an aside I would say that it applies to professors and consultants.)

On a personal note I've found that in many ways excessive talking and not really listening may be culture bound. I've spent a great deal of time in China and noticed how different the Chinese are from Americans in their communication and negotiations skills. Early on the Chinese discovered that if they just waited and kept quiet their American counterpart would feel compelled to fill the silence. He would make more offers, sweeten the deal, or provide incentives - -all to fill that terrible silence. It was just a question of waiting and listening.

The Chinese even have a character to represent the word listening. It has three elements:

a.   listening with our <u>ears</u> – for the verbal message;

b.   listening with our <u>eyes</u> – to observe the nonverbal message;

c.   listening with our <u>hearts</u> –to sense the emotion expressed in the message.

Street Smart Leaders early on find this ultimate core competence –the obsession with listening. The secret to good communication is to TALK LESS AND LISTEN MORE!

# TIPS ABOUT NICHING FROM STREET SMART LEADERS;

- Stay out of the middle. Never take the leader head on. Don't imitate the leading nonprofits or provide similar "me-too" programs or events or activities. (Do we really need another golf tournament, silent auction, or benefit?) Be happy with the nicher position – it's your strength position.

- Narrow your focus to a single problem that you can solve or a unique benefit that you can provide. It would help if you could show some sort of immediate result or "payout" so that your "Power Circle" can be enthusiastic about it. Any program you take on should be natural extension of what you do best. (It's easy to find this out - - ask people; they'll tell you.) REALLY LISTEN!

- Watch that ego trip. Often boards spend a great deal of time and energy competing with other non-profits, or imitating their strategies instead of focusing on their unique mission.   DON'T LET YOUR COMPETITION RUN YOUR BUSINESS OR DICTATE YOUR STRATEGY!

- Leverage your resources (people, time, money, "goodness") behind this area of focus. Become an authority and know everything there is to know about your problem. Make sure local media see you as authority. Practice your story and your elevator speech.

- Take small innovative steps so that if you "fail" it won't be catastrophic. THINK CHUNKING. Be quick to adapt, to grow organically. Be resilient.

- Try Niching through enthusiasts rather than programs. Find evangelists who are like-minded, SHARE YOUR BELIEFS and are willing to spread your story. Let them establish their own networks and spontaneous ways of connecting. Don't forget the advantages of being small, particularly with emerging social media:

- ✓ You can have two-way, interactive communication with your "heavy" user, donor, volunteer, referrer, and supporter.
- ✓ Each member of the Power Circle can have his/her unique chat room, forum, or Facebook page to tell the story of why you're in business.
- ✓ You can do "instant research" by testing offers, programs, ideas etc.
- ✓ You can supplement your resources by getting your storytellers to use their social media.

## CASE 6

# THE DISCONTENTED BOARD WITH THEIR
# NICHER STATUS!

I had been retained by a local teaching hospital to help with their image. The staff and the board, mostly physicians, were concerned with the findings of a recent "share of mind" study. (Respondents are asked to name the hospital that they think of most often!). Hospital L (for Leader) had a 30% rating; two local community hospitals –(C and D) had ratings of 9 and 10%. My client – T – had only a 3 % share of mind.

I tried to explain to the board some of the advantages of a niche position and how 80/20 thinking could make this a viable and successful market position. We could FOCUS on physicians who were alumni of the University; LEVERAGE resources into an online referral, admittance and treatment network for heavy users of the hospital; AND we could MEASURE immediate results of this personalized network for each physician.

Unfortunately my suggestions were to no avail. The staff and board were hung up on their low brand awareness score. They insisted that their staff was every bit as competent and distinguished as the other leading hospitals. They approved a very expensive advertising/public relations campaign featuring their highly skilled and credentialed physicians in dramatic situations within the hospital.

After the year's campaign, they commissioned another share of mind study. They found to their astonishment and acute disappointment that the leading hospital's share of mind  had actually <u>increased</u> to 32%. The competitors stayed relatively the same. But the Teaching Hospital's share had actually gone <u>down</u> to 2%. Follow-up interviews found that respondents had attributed the client's campaign to Hospital L since it was so similar. "It must have been them" was a common response.

## EXERCISE:

How would you describe your niche? (Who are you really? Who do you serve? What do you do that is special? What benefits do you provide? What problem do you solve?)

Are you really different? Google your competition to be sure.

How well do you really listen?

# CHAPTER 7

# THEY ARE GREAT TEAM BUILDERS – THEY FIND THE "VITAL FEW" AND EMPOWER THEM THROUGH POWER CIRCLES.

**"It's amazing how much you can accomplish when it doesn't matter who gets the credit."**
**Harry Truman**

By definition, nonprofits are SHARED POWER ORGANI-ZATIONS. Problems arise when there is an argument as to how best share this power. Peter Drucker reminds us of important differences between nonprofits' governance compared with for profits:

1. Nonprofits have no single bottom line. They have multiple bottom lines and consider everything they do to be righteous, moral and to serve a cause. Therefore, many are unwilling to say that "if it doesn't produce results we should direct our resources elsewhere".

Drucker challenges them to think about "organized abandonment."

2. Nonprofits also have multiple "customers": primary customers - users of the service, and secondary customers – staffs, volunteers, big contributors. He realizes that this word could be controversial among nonprofits but insists that all of these customers can (and do) say no to directions that they don't like. For-profits have only one customer, the buyer, and if the company is public, the stockholder.

3. The "hidden agendas" of board members. These become even more extreme when there are constantly shifting changes with new board members, volunteers coming aboard, new management, etc.

With so many voices to be recognized, the Street Smart Leader quickly focuses on the VITAL FEW – the 20% who contribute most to the nonprofit's success - -however you want to define success. These Vital Few have different names: "shakers and makers", "movers", champions, gatekeepers, influentials - - all reflecting their importance in contributing to that 80%. One thing they have in common is their shared belief as to what makes their nonprofit different!

Successful nonprofits are not built by extraordinary people but "ordinary" people who do extraordinary things together. They've discovered the real secret is that success does not come from the charismatic leader who has all the right answers and who tells everyone what to do but from the Leader who shares his/her belief system and gets others to buy in. Too many bosses would rather be in control than have the organization work well.

As quickly as possible Street Smart Leaders form these Vital Few people into a Power Circle (see Model) that consists of:

A.  Shakers and Movers - - these are the Enthusiasts who have "bought into" the mission of the nonprofit and who really work and accomplish things. They are the 20% who may come from your Volunteers, Staff, Boards, and Donors. They are the "True Believers". They can tell your story, know your Elevator Speech, and can even go through the planning process for their programs.

B.  Special Experts and Resources: depending on strengths of the Shakers and Movers, these are the people who help generate Referrals and can provide special talents. These could be in the media, or promotion agencies, a Webpage Whiz, a faculty member from a local college who could provide students or interns or class research projects or even some consulting.

C.  Allies and Advocates - these people provide access to outreach programs and partnerships with business, media, government and community leaders. Examples of their use could be shared data bases, combined appeals, social networks or advocacy programs.

Street Smart Leaders know that you don't need lots of people, perhaps only 7-12 – <u>if they're the right people</u>.

What motivates them to join the Circle? Remember what we suggested in the chapter on the 80/20 rule: people become active in your organization not necessarily to benefit <u>your</u> organization (altruism) <u>**BUT**</u> for what benefits they get for <u>themselves</u>. What are some of these benefits?

- 9 out of 10 work with your nonprofit because "it enriches my sense of life's purpose" – a particularly strong drive for our aging population.
- Another 9 out of 10 do so for networking and career development (strong among young professionals.)
- Almost three out of four says that it lowers their own personal distress levels and two out of three actually feel better physically.

# SOME TIPS ABOUT POWER CIRCLES:

1.  Use the building blocks of Focus, Leverage and Measurement. Focus on the Shakers and Movers and get them involved in the shared vision and the planning activities. Ideally each should be able to know the business planning process (we presented this in Chapter 5) for their programs or people. Leverage these people and their programs by supporting them with the best "package" of time, money, staff and promotion Measure and keep track of results and feedback into other programs.

2.  Since teams must trust each other, you should expect to engage in "controlled conflict" so that they can see that it is possible to survive. Many people confuse artificial harmony with effectiveness. The key here is not to participate in personal attacks or destructive behavior. In recruiting board members, find those who want to succeed <u>and win</u>, not those who want to <u>be right</u>.

3.  Get in the habit of "chunking" long term missions and goals into shorter-term reachable and achievable objectives so that teams can see rewards and results. Assign responsibilities so that team members can see their role in achievement. CELEBRATE these achievements. Remember that the further away a reward is in the future the smaller the immediate motivation is to attain it.

4.  Expect to come to grips with the 80% who are the "Trivial Many" - - you may not like this term - - perhaps the "non-producing many?" Some may be motivated and retrained but others may have to be treated with "benign neglect" or simply let go. They may just like to see their names

on Boards or lists of Volunteers. A truism about people: <u>Recruit for attitude; train for skills</u>.

On a personal note I always start my consulting stint with locating the Shakers and Movers right away. I have a "no-holds barred" session to see who is "buying" into the overall mission of the nonprofit and their knowledge of the story and elevator speech. Often I find easy-to-implement improvements that they've been reluctant to talk about, which is a tipoff about the nonprofit's culture right there.

Finding these Shakers and Movers is surprisingly easy. Remember the symphony and opera board members that didn't even have season tickets to performances? Hardly a testimonial to their enthusiasm for the importance of their cause.

5. All of the Vital Few should be fundraisers — either via money or in-kind services. Armed with the right Elevator Speeches they should be good solicitors since potential donors ask them how much they contributed themselves.

6. The key to success for a nonprofit is to build from the inside out not outside in, through the Power Circle. It may be slower and perhaps not as dramatic - - as External marketing or promotion campaigns - - but it is the surer way. Recognize that coaching is an on-going process — not something you do with an annual review or bringing in consultants. Your Power Circle will learn more from mistakes than successes because these present "teachable moments."

7. Don't go out into the community unless you have your core group first. Don't promote your nonprofit unless you can live up to expectations. The key is to develop a charismatic organization not the charismatic leader.

## EXERCISE:

If you have a Power Circle, you may have another name for it, fill in the blanks below. If you don't, create one. Review it and write in the names and functions of the members. Then see if it contains the 7-12 people from your various stakeholders who are the high achievers. Note: Do not equate noisemakers or naysayers with achievers.

A.  Who are your Shakers and Movers?

B.  Who are your Special Experts/ Resources?

C.  Who are your Allies and Advocates?

D.  If you don't have a Power Circle, why not?

How good are you at "Chunking"? Translating long term missions into short-term reachable and achievable objectives? Give some examples.

How do you celebrate and recognize attaining these objectives?

What do you want to do with the Trivial Many?

# CASE 7: THE IDEA VILLAGE – POWER CIRCLES

The Idea Village was founded by five entrepreneurs in New Orleans to reverse economic and social decline. They came from marketing, technology and media backgrounds and wanted to create an environment that would encourage talent to stay in New Orleans, grow businesses and create quality jobs. They began using their social and business contacts to transform New Orleans from a city of Brain Drain to a city of Brain Gain.

Building an extensive entrepreneurial network through internal, external and interactive relationships, they now support businesses and create innovative solutions to social challenges. They built a linked network of business, government, legal, and banking and university resources.

This ignited a movement that gave rise to a vibrant, interconnected business support system that includes corporations, non-profits, universities, and government who collaborate to make New Orleans a place for people with big ideas and the passion to build and grow. Culminating with New Orleans Entrepreneur Week, an annual festival of entrepreneurship, it engages global business leaders, students and startup businesses. Over the last twelve years, they have supported 1,800 businesses, connected them to 2,030 professionals and created $100 million in revenue and over 2,000 jobs.

New Orleans is now globally recognized: Forbes named New Orleans the "Biggest Brain Magnet" of 2011 as well as the No. 2 "Best City for Jobs." A July 2010 Brookings Institute "Katrina After 5" report states that New Orleans entrepreneurial activity is 40% above the national average, while Inc. called New Orleans the "Coolest Startup City in America."

# NOTES:

_____

_____

_____

_____

_____

_____

_____

_____

_____

_____

_____

_____

_____

_____

# CHAPTER 8

# THEY HAVE SPECIAL STRATEGIES AND TACTICS WHEN THEIR FUNDRAISING IS NOT RAISING!

**"People don't contribute because of who <u>you</u> are but because of who <u>they</u> are and what they get out of it."**

**Russ Carll, perpetual nonprofit Board Member**

When it comes to such 'bread and butter" issues, Street Smart Leaders tend to use two frames of reference:

1.  As you might expect the 80/20 rule. They know that 80% of their funds will come from 20% of their donors. They also know that they have to focus on the benefits donors gets from contributing to the organization: immediate results and what personal impact they can make.

2. They think STRATEGICALLY and TACTICALLY! The model that I've evolved with some of the leading Street Smart Leaders looks like this:

|  | Appeals/Offers | Appeals/Offers Income Sources |
|---|---|---|
| Current and Past Donors | **Penetration** \*\*\*\*<br><br>Relationships – Loyalty Rewards | **Development** \*\*<br><br>Grants, foundations, Government Contracts |
| New Donors | **Cultivation** \*\*\*<br><br>Testimonials – Referrals from fans | **Diversification** \*<br><br>For Profit Activities |

# TIPS ON FUNDRAISING STRATEGIES:

1. \*\*\*\* As often as possible use a PENETRATION STRATEGY. Do more "business" with your current and former donors. Lock them into some relationship (club membership, support groups, loyalists), recognize them for their loyalty and reward them for their support. The biggest weakness I've found in working with nonprofits is their tendency to take these people for granted and not to thank them or reward them for their efforts. (This is also true of loyal board members and volunteers - - NEVER TAKE THEM FOR GRANTED.) Give them a stake in ownership and convert them into advocates, not only donors or make them a member of the Power Circle.

2. \*\*\* CULTIVATION STRATEGY is next. Remember that it will cost you 4-5 times more to get a new donor than keep an old one. (The old 80/20 rule.) Use testimonials from your current donors and their referrals and give examples of people giving to people, rather than causes. Your Power Circle should be useful here and you can provide them a guide for giving and then show them the immediate results. This is a great place to plug in your customized Social Media "packages".

3. \*\* You might consider a DEVELOPMENT STRATEGY. You will be looking for new sources of income such as grants, foundations, government contracts. I give it lower priority because although they have great potential, they also require special expertise. People could and have written books on the grant writing, special contacts, and often a radical change in mission. The key here would be to have someone in your Power Circle who would champion this strategy and would have the contacts.

My own experience with trying to get grants is that the nonprofits who need them the most - - small size, resources, noble mission - - are least likely to get them. Grants seem to go to the bigger nonprofits skilled in grantsmanship.

4. \* Lastly, the DIVERSIFICATION STRATEGY. This final strategy moves your organization into the for-profit arena. Many museums, art galleries, symphony orchestras/ opera companies have gone this route to supplement their income. Naturally it requires new tax considerations but more importantly it requires a radical change in culture, personnel, and mission.

On a personal note I received an annual report from a local nonprofit recently. To save money - - don't they always? –the PR director tried to do two things: make an annual report and pitch for contributions. I waded through the report and was impressed with all of the brick and mortar improvements, the new facilities, the government grants that they got last year. I even looked at their financials and they seemed to be robust. At the end of the report there was a plaintive request for contributions. My first reaction - - and it continues to this day - - is why should I give them money? They're obviously doing very well and certainly didn't need my contribution.

In looking at these strategies, use the 80/20 mentality: FOCUS ON ONE STRATEGY- don't try to do them all or mix and match. It will probably be PENETRATION - - it's the easiest to LEVERAGE - and certainly you have experience in tracking results. You should have benchmarks from previous campaigns.

If you do decide on another strategy, FOCUS on someone in your Power Circle who has the contacts, and will champion your cause. LEVERAGE your limited resources only on that one goal and AND take small steps that can be easily measured.

Ideally a fund-raising strategy should do more than just solicit funds. It can build a deeper sense of community or increase your share of mind or get public to understand your mission and goals. Your fund-raising should help you get that 15 minutes of fame that you want and deserve.

# TIPS ON FUND RAISING TACTICS

1. In all of your communications focus on the benefits that do-nors get for supporting your organization. Too many nonprof-its talk about themselves, their facilities, operations, people - -WHAT THEY DO - and not what the donors are getting out of it.- WHY THEY DO IT. The more immediate the ben-efits the better. KEEP TELLING YOUR STORY!

2. In most cases people give to people not causes. PEOPLE WHO HAVE SHARED BELIEFS. That's where your Power Circle comes in because they have special reciprocal relation-ships with their contacts. Personal face-to-face communica-tion is still the most powerful form of contact, but it can be extended through social media as well.

3. Expect 80% of your contributions to come from 20% of your board members and volunteers. (The Vital Few.) They should be familiar with your story and have the elevator speech down cold. All support materials should be tailored to their specific needs and styles.

4. Remember that it costs four to five times as much to at-tract a new donor than to keep an old one. (There's that 80/20 rule.) Try to focus on the lifetime value of a donor and see if you can lock this person into a relationship over time. Ask for the repeat gift as soon as possible... within the first three months. Remind the donor of the results or ef-fects of the first gift and show how the second gift can add even more impact. Whenever possible suggest a pathway for future giving that can be tailored to individual's preferences (e.g. payment methods, times, terms, etc.)

5. In talking about contributions such as cash, stock, grants, real estate do not forget about in-kind services. A pro-bono

research study, an outside consulting perspective, a web page expert, a university professor who can provide interns or take on your nonprofit as a class project, can be more useful than "mere" monetary contributions. And never underestimate the contributions of time and energy.

6. ALWAYS, ALWAYS acknowledge the Heavy Donor. Thank them for their contributions and never take them for granted. Usually they have a personal relationship with someone in your Power Circle. Try as much to make contributions reciprocal - - remember they want something back: personal fulfillment, a sense of making an immediate, preferably local impact and RECOGNITION.

7. In summary remember donors love to see where their money goes and what results it achieves. A great example is Donors..org that lets donors customize their gift to a particular school project such as art supplies, field trips, IPads, etc. AdoptA Family.org. focuses on school uniforms for needy students and provides a personalized thank-you note from each recipient.

## WHY DO PEOPLE DONATE? (PUBLIC AGENDA)

Why do people donate? It's mostly emotional; a gut level interest in a cause and faith in people involved. It is a feeling that there are common beliefs that are shared. Very few donations are carefully researched decisions.

Donors are:

People Centered – give to people not institutions- like to have relationships.

Locally Centered - -geographic or psychological.

Seeking immediate benefits

Seeking results, they respond to targets and goals.

Donors give in relation to means and what others give – they need benchmarks.

In general donors look at "slickness" negatively – don't want you to act too much like a profit preoccupied business.

# EXERCISE:

What strategy do you use for fund raising? Which do you find works best for your nonprofit? What's your critical tactic?

Think of your donors as members of your club. They deserve and want two things: Recognition and Special Treatment. Amazon.com, one of the world's most successful companies, is a master of customer recognition. Heavy Users become Prime Members. They get "one- click" ordering (no need to fill out credit card information), no delivery charges, instant videos, suggestions about possible products based on previous selections, etc.

How do you recognize your Loyal Donors? What special treatment do you provide?

## WEBSITE EXERCISE

65% of donors visit the websites of the nonprofits they support – so you have to promote your website. It doesn't generate its own traffic and you have to keep it fresh and updated.

Imagine you're a donor looking at your website. What would it look like? What changes do you see yourself making?

The key to websites is to have "stickiness" the quality of having a visitor "stick" with the website, find out more, perhaps even interact or ask questions. How sticky is your website for donors?

How could you improve its "stickiness"?

Do you feature your Power Circle in your website?

## CASE 8: ANNUAL BISHOP'S FUND APPEAL

This case involved a Catholic Diocese in a Southern Metropolitan City.

A special annual solicitation for the Bishop's Fund was an important source of revenue for Catholic Charities but it started leveling off during the three past years. The first inclination was that the appeal had run its course and was at the end of its Life Cycle (do you remember Chapter 2?) but fortunately a Board Member thought this could be a good candidate for Bottom up Planning.

Two informal research studies were made:

1. A trend analysis over the last three years ranking parishes by how much they contributed to the Bishop's Fund. The 80/20 rule was apparent quickly when it was discovered that a relatively small number of parishes contributed most of the funds. As expected these were parishes with larger populations and affluence. But there were exceptions so...

2. Interviews with Pastors in these exceptional areas revealed two interesting findings: the Priests who did the solicitations were really Champions for the Bishop's Fund and they told stories or related incidents in how the proceeds from the Fund went to help locals in the area deal with family problems, alcohol or drug addiction, returning veterans, etc.

Two positioning strategies were developed for:

1. Pastors of High Performing Parishes—REINFORCEMENT
   – for the first time letters of commendation were sent
   out as well as awards presented at the annual meeting.
   Shortly before the next Bishop's appeal emails were
   sent out as reminders with data about what funds had
   gone to their parishes.

2. Pastors of High Potential Parishes – DEVELOPMENT
   –these received the most attention –they were in parishes with similar demographics but not similar results.
   Pastors or their designates were invited for lunch and
   training sessions were conducted by the Champions
   of High performing Parishes. These demonstrated the
   stories and showed how localized benefits could be
   dramatized. Sample scripts and kits were distributed.
   Elevator speeches were rehearsed.

Results for the next year were heartening. The High
Performing Parishes continued to do well but more importantly the High Potential Parishes started to reach competitive levels.

Ultimately the results of such successful localized programs affected the overall mission of Catholic Charities.
Instead of just talking about Charities for the poor and
needy in the abstract, more emphasis was given to benefits
going to local needs of parishioners.

# NOTES:

_____

_____

_____

_____

_____

_____

_____

_____

_____

_____

_____

_____

_____

# CHAPTER 9

# THEY ARE ADEPT AT POSITIONING (OR IF NEED BE) REPOSITIONING AND USE ELEVATOR SPEECHES

**"If you can't describe your position in eight words or less you don't have a position"**
**Seth Godin**

It might be good to review some the things we know about positioning since it is a fashionable term and lots of people have different, often confusing, definitions.

Positioning is that complex set of perceptions and feelings that "customers" have of your service in relation to the competition. (I purposely use the word customers to be consistent with Peter Drucker's - - primary customers; users, patrons, etc. and secondary; volunteers, board members, and staff.) It forces you to conceptualize how your nonprofit is perceived to be different and superior to competition by providing unique benefits and features.

POSTIONING IS ALL ABOUT PERCEPTION! AND PERCEPTION IS REALITY! For example, more women die from heart disease than all forms of cancer combined. But they perceive heart disease to be an "old man's ailment" from which they are "immune". Just 1 in 5 women realize that heart disease is their number one health threat because they are preoccupied with breast cancer.

Trout and Ries, who are the Fathers of Positioning, suggest some ideas that would be useful to nonprofits.

1. Positioning is all about focus: <u>The more you say the less people hear.</u> To broaden your appeal, narrow your position!

2. Too often people think that if they stand for only one thing they cannot expressly stand for others. They don't understand how the halo effect works: multiple positive associations can relate to a single benefit/characteristic.

3. Perceptions are based on limited first-hand experience and a good deal of second-hand experience (<u>everybody knows</u>!)

4. If you can't be perceived first in a category, create one in which you can. Find that perceptual niche.

Why is positioning important for nonprofits?

There are so many nonprofits competing for attention, volunteers, and funds, customers set up a kind of "pecking order" - - as to their importance and saliency. Customers selectively "see" messages for nonprofits that they like or feel loyalty to; ones that they think share some common beliefs. . In many cases, they don't even see information coming from others. The Breast Cancer perception is a good example.

It is rare for a nonprofit to have one umbrella position since they will have so many different customers seeking different benefits. For example, a Church is not a monolith. Various church goers attend but for different reasons other than just religious motives. Many go because they like the Pastor or minister; some because it is good for the family ; others do so primarily for social reasons - -meeting people, perhaps prospects for marriage; some out of sheer loneliness;. some just like the music, or atmosphere, . (see case at the end of this chapter.)

In a study I did for a symphony orchestra, music appreciation was an important but not critical reason for attending. Many people liked classical music and owned records but did not attend because they were afraid that they would behave inappropriately (applaud at the wrong time), or that they lacked proper attire, or just wouldn't go alone, For many social motivations trumped music - -" it was the thing we did every Friday night and with the same companions. It was like going to church on Sunday "

The best way to dramatize how positioning works is to envision the process as consisting of a triangle of interactive elements:

Your positioning statement consists of three elements:

To: _____

Who could choose _____

I promise _____ (the Elevator Speech, key benefit)

Here are examples of positioning statements:

<u>Tulane University Hospital</u>:

To referring physicians (Tulane Alumni) in the Gulf Coast area...

Who could send patients to Ochsner or Touro Hospitals.

We promise a worry-free, <u>interactive, partnership</u>.

<u>Odyssey House</u>:

To parents and teenagers with drug addictions ...

Who could send them to Bridge House

We can empower them to conquer addiction.

<u>My book</u>:

To decision makers in mostly small nonprofits ...

Who could buy Drucker, Kotler or Levinson (leading authors in the field of nonprofits)

I promise STREET SMART SECRETS WILL HELP YOU THRIVE IN TODAY'S ECONOMY.

Then, the positioning statement is converted into your elevator speech.

## ELEVATOR SPEECHES:

With time and attention so difficult to come by, more and more nonprofit representatives are learning their unique "elevator speech". The term comes from assuming that you meet a prospect (user, donor, media person, politician, etc.) in an elevator. You have only 10 seconds to introduce yourself and get him/her involved in the workings of your organization. (There is actually a dot com "elevator speech" resource if you want to tap into it!)

The most common mistake is to simply tell this person <u>what</u> you do or that you work for or are a volunteer or board member for XYZ nonprofit. It's similar to saying that you are a lawyer, professor, or CPA. In most cases this is a turnoff and the usual response is at best a nod or "that's interesting."

The key is to stress the most important <u>benefit</u> you provide or the critical <u>problem</u> your organization solves from the listener's perspective and WHY it should matter to him or her to listen.

Your elevator speech will be used in everything you do, the tag line in your positioning statement, your web page, when you answer the phone, on your business card. Every member of the Power Circle must learn it by heart and say it naturally.

# NOTES:

_____

_____

_____

_____

_____

_____

_____

_____

_____

_____

_____

_____

_____

_____

# TIPS ON POSITIONING AND ELEVATOR SPEECHES

1.  The best way to find your current position is to <u>ask</u> your stakeholders. At its simplest, ask them when you hear _____ (your name) what do you think of? Ideally you should be hearing something like…..oh! They're the people who do that_____. The key to positioning is the "<u>that</u>".

2.  Remember positioning is what you do to the <u>mind</u> of an individual - - the person who makes the decision - - not to a company or an organization or a government agency. ALWAYS THINK OF A PERSON. You will need different positioning strategies for different target groups. It's really impossible to find one Umbrella Position for everyone.

3.  In trying to reposition your nonprofit you can manipulate three things: the person who (the decision maker); the competitive frame (change the category that you're in); or the difference that makes a difference - - find a new benefit.

    For example, suppose you wanted to reposition your organization from dealing with drug addiction to eating disorders or addictions. You could change the person who makes the decision (it could be parents as well as children); you would now have another group of competitors; and most importantly your difference that makes a difference would have to change substantially.

4.  In repositioning your nonprofit remember there is always a danger of not attracting new customers and losing your old customers. Try to pre-test this change.

5. Your elevator speech and your "difference that makes a difference" can be the same thing. Always be aware of the difference between benefits (why?) and features (what?)

In my case, it took me a while to understand how elevator speeches work. I frequently would meet executives and identify myself as the Director of the Executive MBA program at Tulane. This was usually met by a respectful silence or a nod. After much practice, I came up with a more insightful response: "I run an academic program that increases executives' salaries by 30% in five years." This piqued their interest and they wanted to know more about it.

6. With your elevator speech you should add two ingredients:
Make the person you're talking to feel good – so always use positive framing - - people remember how you made them feel rather than what you said – too many nonprofits harp on negative aspects (the Gloomy Gus approach)

Create the opportunity for follow up – coffee, send information, ask questions, seek feedback advice, business card – always take it to the next level. Suggest resources, create opportunity for a future interaction.

7. Remember in Elevator speeches you engage the <u>heart</u> first (key benefit, problem) - - WHY you are in existence and then engage the <u>head</u> (your system, operation) - - WHAT you do. THINK OF YOUR ELEVATOR SPEECH AS A 10 SECOND HANDSHAKE.

**Some possible elevator speeches for cases discussed throughout book:**

# March of Dimes

We save babies' lives by preventing birth defects, premature births and infant mortality.

## Tom's Shoes

When you buy Tom's shoes you benefit two ways: you get great comfortable shoes and you help a child in need.

## Jitterbug Cell phone

We supply a simple user friendly way to reach out and touch somebody.

## Small Business Administration

We help small businesses survive and make more money

## Fifth Avenue Presbyterian Church

We provide spiritual and psychological comfort throughout your life.

## Smile Train

We help children become whole again – physically and socially.

## Brad Pitt's Make it Right Foundation

We rebuild homes and community spirit.

# Some Thought-Starting Attributes/ Benefits to Be Used In Finding "The Difference That Makes a Difference"

Reliability – accessibility

Ease of contact – client friendly – either voice or technology

Customization – tailoring to client's needs

Skill of contact employees – technical and interpersonal – Politeness, dress code

Consultative talents – Knowledge of clients' problems; anticipation;

Willingness to take on responsibility – guarantee

Credibility – trustworthiness, believability, honesty, integrity, reputation

Technical support – up-to-date equipment, automation, communication

Small size – personal attention, or

Geographical or virtual connections – either localized or contact with other cities, countries, networks.

## CASE 9: THE FIFTH AVENUE PRESBYTERIAN CHURCH – NEW YORK, THE NEED FOR MULTIPLE POSITIONS

The Fifth Avenue Presbyterian Church is a good example of the modern church and the multiple publics it serves and the multiple benefits that it must provide. At the core, there are the religious services you might expect: prayer and worship, presentation of sacraments, holy day observances, etc. but it also provides social, psychological, and financial benefits. The Church is not a monolith and follows the family through its life stages:

For children, it provides day care, religious instruction, illustrated bibles and Easter Egg Hunts.

For young marrieds or singles, there is adult education, parenting classes, lectures, crafts, creative writing, art classes, concerts, and socials. It provides opportunities to be ushers and greeters and serve on various committees. Men's and women's fellowship groups are sponsored.

For older people there are transportation services, large print bibles and hearing enhancements. They can serve on boards of trustees. They are urged to make IRA contributions and contribute securities. Memorials are provided to loved ones. Altruism is encouraged through programs for the homeless; the Bowery and Disaster relief and all church members are asked to volunteer. It provides language classes. Like all nonprofits it must concern itself with fundraising and financial development. Offerings and pledges can be made personally and online.

## EXERCISE:

Positioning

This is the most important exercise you'll be doing in this book. It's your positioning strategy for your own nonprofit.

Let's try two different decision makers. (I'll warn you that B and C must be different for the different Decision Makers.)

Most of my clients have trouble differentiating between two basic concepts: the benefits of a service and its features. Features answer the question: What does your nonprofit do? Benefits answer the questions: What value do I get from this feature? How does it help? What's in it for me? So what?

Sometimes it helps to list the major features of our nonprofit below and then think about these in terms of benefits. Think WIFM- WHAT'S IN IT FOR ME?

# DONORS:

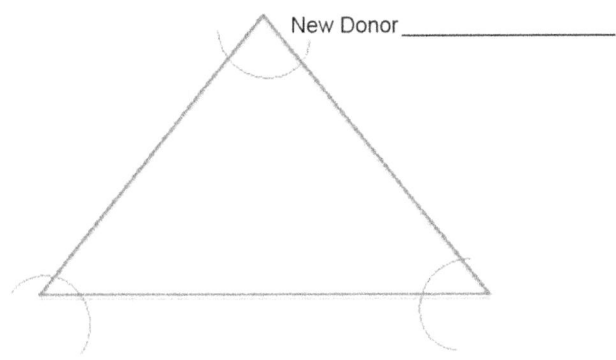

New Donor _____

B. Leading Competitors      C. Difference that makes a difference
(unique benefit to him/her).

## TO THE DECISION MAKER

_____

_____

## WHO COULD CONTRIBUTE TO

_____

_____

## I PROMISE THIS UNIQUE BENEFIT

_____

_____

# BOARD MEMBERS:

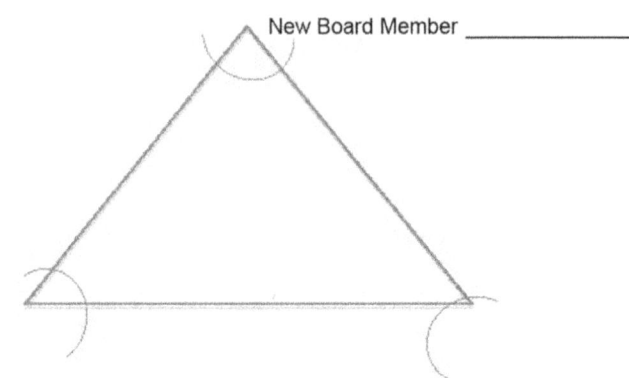

New Board Member _____

B. Leading Competitors

C. Difference that makes a difference
(unique benefit to him/her).

## TO THE DECISION MAKER

_____

_____

## WHO COULD JOIN LEADING COMPETITORS:

_____

_____

## I PROMISE THIS UNIQUE BENEFIT

_____

_____

## EXERCISE:

Write down your elevator speech. Be sure to put the BENEFIT first (Why you do it) and the OPERATION second (How you do it).

Benefit- WHY?

Feature Operation –HOW?

Google your competition and see if your elevator speech is really different. If not, what changes would you make?

Do you use your Elevator speech in everything - - your calling cards, your web pages, your story telling? Why not?

## NOTES:

_____

_____

_____

_____

_____

_____

_____

_____

_____

_____

_____

_____

_____

_____

# CHAPTER 10

# THEY ARE GREAT 'STORY TELLERS' AND WEAVE THEM THROUGH THEIR PROMOTION.

**"YOU ARE YOUR STORY. Work it! He/she who has the best / most compelling, / most resonant/ story wins".**
**Tom Peters**

Back in Chapter 2 we said that STREET SMART LEADERS are great story tellers. They are able to translate their vision of the future internally and externally through pictures, personalities and stories.

The average person today spends <u>8</u> hours a day in front of a screen - - iPhones, iPads, computers, DVD's, game playing, TV watching - - so the challenge is how with limited budgets a nonprofit can <u>pass that screen test</u>. Simply adding to the noise level is not the way.

The key to success is to connect your unique position/ identity with what stakeholders (clients, donors, volunteers, staff) care about AND WHAT THEY BELIEVE. The best way is to tell them a story. A story illustrates how your elevator speech - - your unique benefit or problem solving talent — works to help them. Stories stick with people and work on the right and left brain. They are emotional and compelling. They engage the head and the heart. Stories tell people why you exist, what problems you solve, what benefits you provide and what beliefs you share. PEOPLE CAN REMEMBER STORIES; THEY CAN'T REMEMBER FACTS OR FIGURES.

Hannah Arendt, a political theorist, says that "storytelling reveals meaning without committing to the error of defining it."

The Smile Train's story shows how corrective surgery not only resolves physical problems for young children but helps re-move social ostracism and psychological scarring. Sports4Kids uses its web sites to tell stories about how its programs help transform school yards from places of conflict to organized fun. Families USA features American families sharing everyday problems and struggles with health care.

In their book, The Generosity Network, McRea and Walker suggest that a leader seeking commitment from fol-lowers in a worthy cause should reach out through telling a story. They call it a Public Narrative.

They recommend that all stories be composed of three crucial elements:

- - a story of SELF - - why the leader was called to his/her mission and what are the vision and values that motivate actions;

- - a story of US - - what the constituency or the organiza-tion has been called to - - its shared values and purposes;

- - a story of NOW – the urgent challenges or threats facing they organization and the choices it has to make. It invites the listener to join the cause and to become part of the story.

They remind story tellers to strive for that feeling of <u>connection.</u> That is what moves people to <u>feeling</u> and from feeling to <u>action.</u>

Stories can be powerful motivators for the Power Circle as well. Faced by perceptions that a nonprofit is too small  or just a one person operation, it's easy to remind the "Doubting Thomas" that in the for profit world the late Steve Jobs of Apple, Bill Gates of Microsoft and Jeff Bezos of Amazon started their businesses in their garage. Howard Schultz helped transform a small coffee company out of Seattle, Starbucks, into the largest coffeehouse company in the world.

<u>A jewel</u>  of a book for Street Smart Leaders loaded with inspirational stories for smaller nonprofits is Malcolm Gladwell's recent <u>David and Goliath</u>.  His basic theme is that ordinary people can take on and beat giants. Contrary to conventional wisdom, David's <u>size</u>, skill and agility really made him superior to Goliath's bulk and ponderousness. Gladwell shows data that two-thirds of "weaker" countries over the years have defeated powerful stronger countries IF they don't fight by the same rules. They use unconventional guerrilla tactics.

So-called disabilities can force people to develop skills that might have lain dormant. He cites cases of Richard Branson, British billionaire and entrepreneur, Charles Schwab, founder of discount brokers, and Paul Orfalea, CEO of Kinkos, were all dyslexic. Because of this "disability" they developed skills and attitudes to compensate like listening better or dealing with failure or daring things that they might not have otherwise considered.

Gladwell supports the theme that advantages may actually be disadvantages. For example, going to a less elite school or less privileged environment may give you more freedom to pursue your own ideas and academic interests.

Nonprofits are rich with inspirational stories also. Mohammed Yunus won the 2006 Nobel Prize. He defied conventional logic by loaning to the poorest of the poor without collateral in rural Bangladesh. Yunus showed that good business and social benevolence often pursued separately could be combined successfully.

These stories can be also visual. TV viewers of MSNBC can see almost weekly vignettes of a successful partnership between Lawrence O'Donnell and UNICEF providing desks to children in Milawi through the ground-breaking KIND program — kids in need of desk. The program has been extended to scholarships for young girls.

The world is rich with stories! They just have to be mined and polished by Street Smart Leaders.

# SOME TIPS FROM STREET SMART LEADERS

1. Translate your elevator speech into a story. Look for an emotional hook to help the audience connect with the story. Always think of benefits and problems solved and/ or COMMON BELIEFS! Then get interested others to tell that story for you. It's the cheapest and most effective form of communications. Remember that when you try to persuade someone, you're automatically suspect - - you're trying to get someone to accept something or some idea. Getting a Third Party, someone who is disinterested, is always more powerful.

2. The best stories START with WHY you help – and then back them up with the <u>what</u> and the <u>how</u>. Promote from the inside out and not outside in. Start with your Power Circle, empower them to communicate, making sure they know your elevator speech cold and tell <u>your unique story</u>. Remember these are the "inspired evangelists", who share your beliefs with their own special communities of interest. Also they can leverage social media to interact and engage with these people.

   If you can't get your Power Circle to do this job, it may be time to STOP AND FIND A NEW POWER CIRCLE. If you can't get your internal team to be enthusiastic, what do you think external publics will be? <u>There is nothing magic about communication</u>.

3. Organize ways to collect stories. Your web page is one of the best ways – be sure to feature them and offer awards for best stories.

   In addition to "real people" using famous personalities helps stories stand out: Jimmy Carter's work with Habitat for

Humanity, Brad Pitt's role in rebuilding New Orleans after Katrina. After many years I still associate President Franklin Roosevelt with the March of Dimes and polio. The most credible story tellers however, are "real people", families and friends.

4. Whenever possible use the AIDA formula for telling your story.

   A - - ATTENTION. Am I getting the right audience interested in my STORY? I do this through a promised benefit or problem that I'm solving.

   I - - INTEREST. This is the AHA! Response - this is me that you're talking to!

   D - -DESIRE. This is when people mentally rehearse what you're suggesting. I see myself enjoying the benefit, solving the problem or contributing.

   A - -ACTION. What do you want me to do now? Write, click, find a web page, give, call someone? THIS ACTION STAGE IS KEY BECAUSE IT IS THE WAY TO YOU WILL TRACK RESULTS.

5. Remember that your brand is your story to the world! It should evoke positive emotion when people hear it and see it! A tell-tale sign of problems with your brand is when your stakeholders have a tough time explaining what you do and what you stand for. That means they don't know your story.

## EXERCISE:

What is your nonprofit's story? Does it pass the AIDA test?

If you don't have a story, make one up!

Do all of your Power Circle know your story and can they tell it well? Who else is telling your story?

## EXERCISE:

THINK SMALL EXERCISE —Telling your story in small space.

Your most useful Street Smart promotional piece that everyone in your Power Circle and staff should have is your Business Card. It should always serve double duty: identification - your various addresses, including your website, name, location, phone; and TELLING YOUR STORY _ your elevator speech, that tag line that differentiates you from all of the others. It should be an extension of your web page, preferably using similar colors, themes, and ideas. Take a look at your current card and make improvements now and remember AIDA.

| Your Current Business Card | Improvements |
| --- | --- |
|  |  |

THINK BIG EXERCISE –telling your story in large space.

Now convert your small business card into a sign, one you will use at your annual meeting, or as a large poster, or to head your web page. How do you tell your story VISUALLY? The key is what you will have to leave out. Don't forget identification and positioning and AIDA.

| Your Current Web Page | Improvements |
|---|---|
|  |  |

## NOTES:

# CHAPTER 11

# THEY VALUE THEIR BRAND EQUITY AND USE IT IN ALL OF THEIR PROMOTION.

**"Branding is mostly about answering the question: "so what does that have to do with me?"**

**Levinson, Adkins and Forbes.**

In the first chapter, we showed how the March of Dimes was able to reposition its organization from one concerned with children with polio to one concerned with birth defects, premature births and infant mortality.

They were able to do that because of their powerful brand. In the for profit world, some brands like Coca Cola, Apple, Mercedes Benz, Starbucks, have actually been valued in monetary terms in millions of dollars. The same thing could be done for the Red Cross, or Salvation Army or American Heart Association. Brand Equity is defined as the <u>additional value that a brand name adds to an otherwise equivalent product or service</u>.

Brands and branding have become quite fashionable of late. (You can even get companies that will help you create your own personal brand for employment purposes.) Consequently there is considerable confusion. Branding isn't just about getting people's attention or using it in integrated communication. It is a powerful guide, helping people know how to think of you and how to remember you. <u>It is a promise of quality and performance</u>. As such it offers a perpetual challenge to deliver on that promise. Your brand tells your story to the world.

Some of the larger nonprofits practice Philanthropy Branding- - fitting the issue to the person's personality: Angelina Jolie with refugees, Bono with AIDS, George Clooney with Darfur. As usual the key is credibility and a perceptual identity.

A strong brand does the following:

1.  Defines your organization's values – what you stand for! It is perceptual shorthand of your "elevator speech". Ultimately your brand is what <u>other</u> people say.

2.  Promotes being unique, standing out, being distinctive. This is probably the hardest problem for nonprofits. (In New Orleans we have Odyssey House, Bridge House, and Grace House - - all dealing with addictions!)

3.  Represents your niche – your function – your beliefs!

4.  Triggers memories of your unique story.

In sum, a good brand is similar to a reputation for a person and can forge connections and create relationships with different stakeholders. But building brands that meet all of these attributes can be a very expensive proposition. Be aware that some nonprofits donors may feel that too much money is spent simply enhancing brands (the Madison Avenue syndrome).

# STREET SMART TIPS FOR BRANDING:

1. Monograms are for shirts not for your nonprofit.

   Too many nonprofits try to imitate for profits trend toward using initials or monograms to represent their companies. (Blame IBM?) And there are lots of identity companies who love to create identity or image programs at substantial costs based on new initials or acronyms for nonprofits. Some nonprofits over the years have been successful the YMCA, the AARP, and PTA) but in general monograms are confusing. People don't have the time or patience to figure out what each letter stands for. Acronyms lack memorability; they offer no promise of reward; and especially for nonprofits, they lack humanity.

   Any guesses as to what IBS, OIC, OHL, or NHS stand for? These were taken from a list of New Orleans social service organizations.

2. All nonprofit brands or names could be strengthened by using tag lines.

   Because so many nonprofits brand names are so similar (remember all of those Houses mentioned previously?) almost all could benefit from a tag line - - sometimes called a theme line – which is a shorthand version of your elevator speech.

   Examples:

| March of Dimes | Saving Babies Together |
|----------------|------------------------|
| Odyssey House | Empowering People to Conquer Addiction |

| Greater Good Network | Shop Where it Matters |
|---|---|
| Goodwill | Let's Go to Work |

Brad Pitt's Make it Right Foundation has as its mission to rebuild homes wiped away by the levee failure in New Orleans' Ninth Ward at the time of Hurricane Katrina. The Name "Make it Right" has a powerful double meaning - -not only to rebuild strong houses but also to preserve the spirit of that community's unique culture.

Could it be stronger if some sort of tag line were added to indicate more the purpose and locale of the Foundation?

3. Generic names encourage generic business! If possible don't choose a name that describes something that everybody does. The key is how much valuable information PER INCH does your name imply? Brands confer power to customers and usually relate to emotions from childhood. (I will always remember the March of Dimes and the Mothers' March!)

Brand equity is the financial value of brand loyalty. It costs 4-6 times more to convert a new user, volunteer, and donor than it does to retain one. Keeping a satisfied donor, user, and volunteer costs only about 1/5 as much as attracting a new one.

4. Because the Internet is so important today, all Brand Names should have some domain link in their names.

Since almost all nonprofits have their own web sites it would pay to have your brand and your web address coordinated.

Having your own unique URL makes you look more credible to search engines. It is a way for you to carve out a unique place in cyberspace.

5.  Your Web address may be more important than your physical address. Make sure your site is current and "sticky" (i.e. encouraging viewers to stick around and preferably to look in each day to see what they're missing). REMEMBER on this site you are the authority – the main source for information and tips. If possible make your site interactive and get members of your Power Circle to interact.

6.  In this noisy and visual age, more and more nonprofits are using MEMES to tell their stories and unify their promotion.

    MEMES (rhymes with themes) are visual shorthand symbols or personalities that can be used as spokespersons for your nonprofit. They can be human (Brad Pitt, Paul Newman) or cartoon characters (Smokey the Bear, McGruff, the Crime Dog) or symbols (the Red Cross, I Heart NY) or even colors (pink for breast Cancer).

# STREET SMART TIPS ON PROMOTION

1. Your Brand is what integrates all of your promotion. The 80/20 rule applies to your communication and promotion. FOCUS on what people, appeals, programs are working and get rid of those that are not. LEVERAGE all of your resources (people, money, and image) behind these programs. MEASURE, and track results and effectiveness. Remember the poorest reason for having a fancy brochure, new logo or a web site is because others have them or they're bigger than we are so " they must know."


2. Make your limited budgets work harder.

   DOMINATE —a time, a season, an event. Every group/person has its 15 minutes of fame, what is yours?

   INNOVATE - - find new and interesting ways to promote and communicate your story and brand. Tailor them to your Power Circle.

   CONCENTRATE - - all of your resources on what's working and create "packages"

   COOPERATE - - find like-minded nonprofits as well as business partners with common interests, missions and goals. Think about strategic alliances, coordinated events, fund-raising, etc.

3. Take a look at the promotional tools available to your nonprofit. Don't be overwhelmed. Remember to always use your 80/20 rule and focus on the ones that you think are giving you your "biggest bang for a buck". Concentrate on the ones that your Power Circle can use effectively to reach their audiences. Each should be a master of at least one medium that most

effectively tells your story. Remember that each member will have a different personal style, contacts and tools with which they are comfortable- - you need to tailor what they need. .

You might want to think in terms of good, better, and best "packages." For example, a GOOD package might be business cards, reprints of your story, basic elevator speech, Facebook listing. . A BETTER package might add your annual report, reprints from your web page, a specialty item. The BEST package might involve special events, workshops, co-branding with cause-related partners. It's really a question of style and budget.

The following table shows most of the promotional tools available to nonprofits. It includes the maxi or mass media as well as the mini or more selective media. You might take a couple of minutes to acquaint yourself with the various tools and perhaps even check the ones that you're using now.

## PROMOTIONAL TOOLS FOR NON-PROFITS

| Max/Mass Media | |
|---|---|
| Advertising<br>Print-Newspaper,<br>Magazines, Supplements<br>Bradcast – TV, Radio<br>Outdoor, Billboards,<br>Transit<br>Institutional Advertising<br>– Advocacy, Cause<br>Related, Fusion | Public Relations/publicity<br>News releases, media kits, DVDs,<br>Articles<br>Social Events – Seminars,<br>Workshops,<br>Article, sponsorships, sports. co-<br>branding, news conferences<br>Public Service<br>Announcements – cause related<br>Barter |

| Mini/Selective Media | |
|---|---|
| Logos, Business Cards Direct Mail, Annual Reports, Newsletters, Cyberspace, Telemarketing- Directories<br><br>Support for Volunteers, Donors, Contest, Sweepstakes, gifts, Premiums. Specialties<br><br>Tradeshows/ Conventions | **EMedia/Social Media**<br>Websites, Blogging<br>Podcasting<br>YouTube<br>iTunes<br>Twitter<br>Viral Media |

# CASE 10: DO YOU REALLY NEED A NEW LOGO?

As a consultant I find often that management equates busyness with effectiveness. They take on lots of low resistance items that give them an excuse to avoid having to deal with the more challenging and high resistance items.

Being "overwhelmed" is often an escape mechanism for not really tack-ling important issues such as relevant missions, achievable goals, having unique position.

In one case there was a vendetta between the new chairman of the board - a retired businessman - -and the nonprofit's CEO. The Chairman constantly complained about the CEO's financial accounting skills even though the CEO was originally recruited because of his prowess in getting grants and his government contacts. Often my appointments to visit with the Board were scheduled when one or the other was unavailable so that things would go more "smoothly."

The constant bickering was quieted for a while when the group decided to get a new more "up-to-date" logo that would make them look more modern. This kept the board busy looking at various designs for months without having to resolve a more critical issue. Worse yet, the new logo just confused people and a good deal of brand equity was lost.

## EXERCISE:

Look at the attributes of a good brand. How do you think your brand stacks up?

Are you using a tag line? If not, what would yours look like?

Pick out two of your best story tellers and create a package of promotional tools that you think they would need to tell your story.

Look at your web site. Is it "sticky"?

What do you do each year to get your "15 Minutes" of Fame?"

# NOTES:

_____

_____

_____

_____

_____

_____

_____

_____

_____

_____

_____

_____

_____

# CHAPTER 12

# THEY REALIZE THAT THEIR SUCCESS DEPENDS ON BUILDING, KEEPING LONG TERM RELATIONSHIPS AND PRESERVING BRAND LOYALTY...

**"The secret is how you translate a casual affair into a long-term marriage."**

**Ted Levitt**

Ultimately nonprofits can be seen as a network of <u>beneficial relationships</u>. The following model shows how these relations develop and can serve as a review of points discussed in previous chapters.

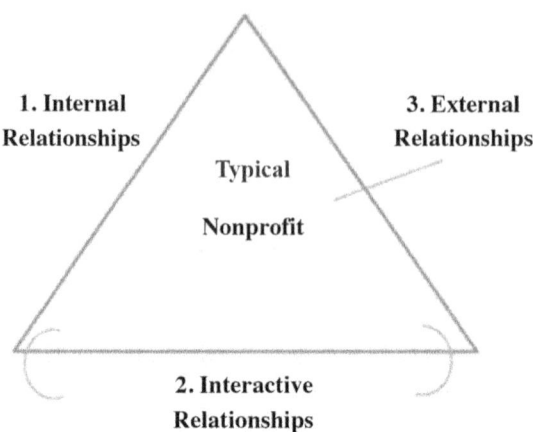

1. Internal relationships - -In chapter 7, we talked about the Power Circle - - the guiding coalition of people committed to the organization. These are the Vital Few (the 80/20 group) that are recruited, energized and have "bought into" the mission of the nonprofit. They can tell the Story and know the Elevator Speech backwards and forwards.

2. Interactive relationships - -the Power Circle has its own constituencies with which it develops relationships - - both High Tech – through on line or social media - - or High Touch –through personal interactions. This group is enabled and empowered to cultivate referrals and to produce long term results. The Street Smart Leader is comfortable in letting 1 and 2 do as much of the heavy lifting as possible.

3. External relationships - - these deal with outreach programs and strategic alliances or partnerships with businesses, media, government or community leaders. These can involve on line social networks, shared data bases, cooperative funding drives, etc. The Street Smart Leader knows that you don't go into this external "community" unless 1 and 2 are working efficiently,

The "secret" is to engage people at all three levels to help build the organization and accomplish its goals. The emphasis throughout is on building and keeping <u>long term relationships</u> rather than one-time transactions. To a great extent the Street Smart Leader becomes a master in managing relationships and building and retaining loyalty.

In the Generosity Network, McRea and Walker, eloquently insist that relationship building and not money is at the heart of social activism. They challenge fundraisers to shift from "asking for help" to exploring how both parties can work together in pursuit of a common vision with the resources that both parties have to offer.

Their basic theme is that true generosity is rooted in relatedness. They insist that fund raising is just not about meeting dollar quotas or targeted results on annual appeals but MAKING A DIFFERENCE THROUGH CREATIVE HUMAN CONNECTIONS. These connections are based on people's willingness to dedicate themselves to causes that change their self-image and make their lives richer.

Street Smart Leaders understand that one of their most important relationships will be with other smaller nonprofits. It has been said that the greatest strength of a nonprofit is its willingness to go it alone. Unfortunately this is often the greatest weakness.

Many pay lip service to the need for working with other nonprofits for the "greater good" but often they see themselves competing with others for scarce resources, such as volunteers, funds and community awareness.

Too often board members (names not revealed to protect the guilty) suffer from this form of myopia. I've seen examples of nonprofits not sharing mailing lists even though clienteles are similar, or of refusing to merge boards in face of declining demand or duplicate membership.

As one Street Smart Leader suggested "in the long run we need to grow the pie instead of grabbing our own slice."

The most effective Leaders work in informal coalitions or networks.(interpersonal or online.) They share knowledge through research and publications. They build skills through training and workshops. They recognize the need to share their most important resource and asset – their people.

## SOME TIPS ABOUT RELATIONSHIPS:

1.  Too many managers get involved with building external relationships rather than cultivating the Internal and Interactive relationships first. You cannot give what you don't have.

    (A story told by one of the Street Smart LEADERS is relevant here. When airlines make announcements about using air masks in case of sudden loss of pressure in the cabin, they remind mothers that they should take care of their oxygen mask first before taking care of their child. It points out the value of establishing priorities.)

2.  One of your most effective relationships will be with people who make referrals. Too often they are a "forgotten opportunity". Contrary to popular opinion people like to give referrals and don't have a sense of being bothered. Humans are wired to making referrals since it gives them a deeply satisfying way to connect with others. They see themselves as "inside dopesters" with unique contacts and special expertise. (See case on Power of Referrals)

    A truism is that one referred client, volunteer, or board member is worth five that might come through promotion or mass media.

    Street Smart LEADERS use their Internal and interactive groups to generate referrals and they coach their Power Circle to ask for referrals. To a great extent a good referral network was the first social network. Once you get a referral these people are to be thanked, kept informed of the results of their referral, and as much as possible integrated into the Vital Few.

3.  If at all possible combine the best of High Tech connections with High Touch Engagement. Remember that 1 PLUS 1 = 3.

High tech connections - Web Pages, Internet, Social Media - - are ideal for making contact, giving out information, learning about your story, keeping people in the informational loop, etc. . High Touch engagement - - human contact and personal follow up - -help to build trust, offer opportunities for customizing appeals and reinforce relationships. Don't depend on Twitter or Facebook to develop a powerful relationship.

On a personal note I've given to several nonprofits who are very efficient with high tech - - I can be billed automatically for annual contributions for example – but who have never contacted me personally even by phone to tell me about the results of their effort. I gather they expect me to seek out their web page. Others overly depend on high touch - - personal solicitations – that could be done much more efficiently through high tech.

4. Loyal "customers" (Drucker's term for all stakeholders) are "more profitable" (beneficial, cost effective) than "one-shot" customers. They cost less to serve since you have information and data about their habits. You can tailor your appeals and your services. It is possible to "lock them" into a relationship - - you can calculate the Lifetime Value of a loyal donor. They can be great referral agents to tell your story and give testimonials. Lastly, they make great volunteers and board members.

5. Good relationships provide these benefits to shareholders and should be used in all promotion:

    • Confidence - - there is less anxiety about choosing the "right charity"- or knowing what is best. Most people have a "pecking order" of acceptable charities and a long-term relationship makes it easier.

- Social benefits - -it is possible to know the Vital Few people by name - - some become an extended family.
- Special treatment - - by becoming a frequent donor, buyer, user one can be extended special priorities or extra services.

6. The key to all relationship networking — PEOPLE DO BUSINESS WITH PEOPLE THEY LIKE!

# EXERCISE:

Relationships

Using the model of relationships how well are you doing in setting up your internal, interactive and external relationships? Who are the key players? Who is the Power Circle?

Have you done a good job of taking care of your internal relationships before you worry about external relationships? (Remember that Oxygen Mask.)

# CASE 11: TULANE UNIVERSITY'S EMBA PROGRAM

# THE POWER OF REFERRAL! THE 80/20 RULE IN ACTION!

After the first years of growth, the enrollment of the Executive MBA program of the A. B. Freeman business school plateaued. We had filled the pipeline of prospective executives and the program's newness had "worn off".

We used the 80/20 rule and focused on the various promotional and marketing tools we had used in previous years. We tracked results and expenses of advertisements in business magazines and newspapers; open houses; direct mail solicitations; and referrals of business alumni from the previous years. We found that referrals had cost only 20% of the budget but gave us 80% of our qualified candidates. The other sources gave us more "bodies', but referrals did a better job of pre-selecting candidates and building up reasonable expectations.

We set up alumni groups from each class, and each alum was personally solicited to set up appointments at his/her company and encouraged to be present. We found they did the best job of selling the program. We set up a follow up program to thank executives for their recommendations.

We reduced promotion expense and found that the referral program became self -sustaining. We found that 20% of the sponsoring companies accounted for 80% of the candidates.

# PART III
# WHERE DO WE GO
# FROM HERE?

# CHAPTER 13

# WHAT DO STREET SMART LEADERS PREDICT FOR THE FUTURE?

As you might expect, their views about issues are similar to the story about the Blind Men and the Elephant. Each Leader sees the world in a different way because of different perspectives and the wide range of nonprofits. Some important issues:

## VOLUNTEERS

My experience is that very few of the nonprofits - - maybe one in 10 - -do a good job of aligning the tasks they assign to volunteers with their specific skills. Most managers focus mostly on financial or in-kind contributions rather than volunteers' willingness to work or the set of skills they bring to the nonprofit. For example, so many still youngish executives are retiring and bring in management, technological and consulting aptitudes. They are looking for a way to make a difference in their lives and many see nonprofits as offering that way. Once the children are grown, women still have that creative urge to do something useful. They have great multitasking skills and would seem to be natural leaders for nonprofits. And of course there are always young people looking for causes and community projects. We really haven't tapped this reservoir and the volunteer is really still the unique symbol of nonprofits.

# SOCIAL MEDIA

I heard a colleague say that now with social media, if you don't have anything to say, you now have thousands of ways to say it. There is no doubt that the future of nonprofits and social media are intertwined. Members of the Power Circle will now have their own ways to tell our story to their different constituencies. They can choose Face Book, Twitter, Linked in, and You Tube to tailor their messages AND most importantly interact with key target audiences. Also we'll be able to use these social media for quick research studies and get immediate feedback from stakeholders about some of our programs and people. That way we keep adjusting our strategies and focus on what's working. Who knows some day we'll worry less about Brick and Mortar solutions and think of cyber networks.

Nonprofits use <u>social media</u> to share ideas, content, thoughts and relationships on line. This sharing can be done with other like-minded nonprofits and with government and businesses.

Social media differ from mainstream media in that anyone can create, comment on or add to the information flow via text, audio, video, images and communities. (Some people use the term social networking.) We can all be instant publishers.

Social media can help to shape conversations as well as allow us to participate. We can monitor what other people are saying about us or comment on other blogs. The implications for nonprofits would seem endless.

We can:

1. Bypass normal institutions like family, school, neighbor-hoods, businesses and go directly to our audiences irre-spective of location. (We can even be global).

2. Track giving habits, performance, frequency, amounts. We can develop recommendation engines.

3. Coordinate with other nonprofits of comparable size, sim-ilar donor bases – electronic United Ways - -as well as share mutual missions, goals, programs and facilities. Set up strategic partnerships.

4. Leverage every member of the "Power Circle" to tell the story using his/her favorite medium.

THE INTERNET – WELCOME TO THE CONNECTIONS ECONOMY!

The internet is a "virtual city". People commute <u>online</u> rather than in the "normal fashion." The average internet user spends two hours per day shopping, paying bills, being informed or entertained. 40% of Americans will have consulted a web page during the typical day. Brick and mortar establishments become electronic screens for the Amazons, e-bays and Craig list.

There are lots of stereotypes about Internet Usage. It is not just used by young people or males. Women make up 45% of the users and they are the vast majority of social networking sites (except for LinkedIn). Women between

30-50 are the biggest users of online dating, financial services, and medical information.)

Increasingly our natural habitat is online and we seem to have an insatiable appetite for information, affiliation and connection. This trend has natural repercussions. News is flourishing but not in newspapers. Contacts are increasing but not interpersonally. Social media have become dominant. Control has moved from the sender to the receiver.

Our web page makes us equal to the largest competitors, but we have to promote our website. It doesn't generate its own traffic and it must be updated regularly.


## WE'LL HAVE TO DO MORE CHUNKING!

I never knew too much about this concept until I understood that the key to success for a nonprofit is to demonstrate to your Power Circle that they can succeed with <u>short term</u> wins. For example when I worked with the American Lung Association years ago our mission was "dedicated to prevention and control of lung diseases and related causes. Our goal was to be publicly recognized as the premier public health agency for lung health related issues." Certainly this was noble and a very ambitious and long range mission.

But how do we demonstrate that we're really moving in the right direction? How do we keep people motivated and with a sense of urgency? The best way I've learned is chunking - - breaking long-range goals into small steps that can be achieved, measured and rewarded. And I use it in my nonprofit particularly when it comes to the business planning process. I focus on programs that are highly visible and clearly related to our overall mission. By chunking I automatically build a sequence where I don't try to do many things at one time or try to skip steps. I find that success in chunking counters cynics and resisters and helps build momentum.

## STRATEGIC PARTNERSHIPS OR THE URGE TO MERGE!

Most nonprofits have been loners –they often pride themselves on being able to succeed on their own. But the future will have to depend on setting up strategic partnerships, or less grandly, find ways to merge or cooperate. I've always worked on the formula that 1 + 1 =3. But of course you have to be careful with whom you're merging or partnering. Right now, American divorces and mergers have about the same success rate - - about 50%! The key is to find partners that you can trust, are compatible, provide supplementary expertise and are flexible. The right merger partners can provide economies of size and scale. With them you can share web sites, events, fund-raising, even such specializations as research, or marketing, or using consultants. Nonprofits can also set up partnerships with businesses via co-branding or joint advocacy projects.

## WE HAVE TO WORK SMARTER NOT HARDER.

I know it's a cliché but it's still appropriate. I find that lots of my colleagues brag about how much time they spend on the job or how stressed their jobs make them. Too many equate busyness with effectiveness. I like what Henry David Thoreau says: "It's not enough to be busy. So are the ants. The question is what are we busy about."

The best thing to do is to apply that 80/20 rule to your management style and your own job performance.

We've got to learn to say <u>No</u> to all those board meetings, or placating naysayers or trouble makers. Success is what you don't do. Warren Buffet says that "for every 100 great opportunities brought to me I say no 99 times." The bugaboo seems to be multitasking. Steve Uzzell says that multitasking is merely the excuse to screw up more than one thing at a time.

## WE HAVE TO BUILD LIAISONS WITH COLLEGES AND UNIVERSITIES, PARTICULARLY BUSINESS SCHOOLS.

Now that Social Entrepreneurship is fashionable at Colleges and Universities we have special opportunities to get faculty members on our Boards or to serve as consultants. They are a great source for getting students and classes for projects. Also many have skills to help us with computers, data bases, social networking, and building web sites. Many schools offer class competitions and are looking for nonprofits to serve as "guinea pigs." Perhaps we could get members of our Power Circles to sponsor class competitions or provide scholarships or internships for their students. We shouldn't forget community colleges with older students who can provide us with prospective volunteers and employees.

## MICRO-MANAGING.

We should be careful of micromanaging particularly by boards.. I was on a board that had recruited a great rainmaker and grant writer as manager, but instead of respecting that talent they kept complaining about his operational skills. It would have been easier and cheaper to hire an adminstrative assistant and let the manager do what he did best.

Leaders may initiate an activity or program but it takes a group of fanatics who make it a movement. Drucker says that "90% of management consists of making it difficult for people to get things done." That's where our relatively small size helps. We shouldn't be afraid of making mistakes. Long term successes come from short-term focuses. We should realzie that we should not only celebrate the touchdowns but the first downs also.

## NONPROFITS AND REINVENTION!

Nonprofits need to reinvent themselves. In today's world the only constant is change. We've always been good in changing others - - their ideas, attitudes and behavior - - but we've been slower in changing ourselves. We should recognize that growth is not a steady linear pattern but really a culmination of cycles - -ups and downs, positives and negatives, joys and sorrows. Some of these cycles come about externally: economic downturns like the ones we're having right now; new confusing competition; and impacts of the new technology. Some come about internally; loss of leadership, losing focus on primary mission, settling into a comfort zone. We should learn to <u>embrace</u> change and <u>not fear</u> it. We should understand that growth is a constant pattern of reinvention. Even obstacles can be seen as opportunities for growth, to create something new based on the old.

## WE HAVE TO LEARN FROM OUR MISTAKES!

We have to learn that success always starts with failure. I've got a three-step recipe for adapting. We should always be willing to try new things with the expectation that some will fail. I once read a Prussian General's comment that "no plan survives first contact with the enemy. What matters is how quickly the leader is able to adapt." We should always make failure survivable because it will be so common. And when we've failed we should move on and not continue to pour money into something that's not working. We keep telling other to change but we seem to be reluctant to do so. One big problem is letting competitors rule our life. Too many nonprofits overly concern themselves with outdoing their fellow nonprofits rather than trying to find their own identity.

## WE HAVE TO CHANGE IMAGE OF NONPROFITS!

We will never become a dominant force in American lives until we get rid of the misconception that overhead for nonprofits is wasteful and bad while it is perfectly ok for the for profits! Somehow people have been brainwashed to believe that a good nonprofit is one that works with the smallest overhead percentage. Having different charity rating systems focusing on this measure doesn't help. Most of us are being starved for resources. Dan Pallota's book, Uncharitable,, highlights the Catch 22 we're in. Our employee compensation packages are far lower than the for profits. which means it's harder to attract top executives. We're restricted in how much we can put into advertising and marketing while that's not the case for the for profits. And strangely enough funders have longer time frames for investing in the for profits while they expect us to show results in shorter times. It's like we're living in two different worlds. The for profit companies brag about how much they're investing in new technology and equipment and customers think it's great because it adds value. For them that's GOOD OVERHEAD. But for us all overhead seems to be wasteful and bad. These perceptions have to change if we're to grow. I've always found it curious that we're in business of changing views about difficult issues but we don't seem to be able to do this about ourselves.

# GETTING BIGGER IS NOT ALWAYS BETTER!

This may seem sacrilegious but perhaps we ought to focus on just being BIG ENOUGH and not always worrying about getting bigger and bigger. For me growth comes from running my nonprofit well and should not be a goal in itself. Why do we have to be the biggest nonprofit in our area or in our category? I've seen too many nonprofits growing too fast and this has detracted from their core purpose. Nonprofit people should do what they love but too often we get bogged down in managerial details. What's wrong with being BIG ENOUGH? That helps keep our freedom and yet we can still focus on our special purpose - - that's why we came into nonprofits in the first place.

## NOTES:

_____

_____

_____

_____

_____

_____

_____

_____

_____

_____

_____

_____

_____

# CHAPTER 14

# SOME FINAL THOUGHTS – HOW CAN STREETS SMARTS HELP IN THE FUTURE?

Having reached the "second half" of my life and observed all of the "crises" and predicted changes brought about by new technology and competition over the years I have always taken comfort in the familiar French quote by Jean Baptiste Alphonse Karr, a French journalist:

"Plus ca change, plus c'est la meme". (The more things change, the more they stay the same.)

For purposes of this book, I've taken the liberty of paraphrasing:

"The more things (the environment, competition, technology) change, the more they (street smart attitude and skills) stay the same.

The same traits and talents that helped Street Smart nonprofits grow and prosper during the past and present will be even more useful in the future. Let's briefly review these predicted challenges and how Street Smart nonprofits can react.

- <u>Nonprofits will have to keep changing and reinventing themselves.</u>
- <u>The world will become even noiser with higher sound barriers.</u> Instead of just joining in with the noise, it will become more important to really listen to what stakeholders want. With the new interactive social media it should be easier to get feedback. And each member of the Power Circle will have his/her own communication network.
- <u>The challenge of new technology</u> - - the "high tech" - - will have to be counterbalanced by "high touch" ways of connecting with people through building connections and relationships. THE MORE WE ARE CONNECTED ELECTRONICALLY THE LESS WE ARE CONNECTED PHYSICALLY AND EMOTIONALLY. The most important relationships will be INTERNAL with the Power Circle working outwards. The magic words will be collaboration, participation and collective action; partnerships with other nonprofits as well the other two sectors: government and private.
- <u>There will be even more nonprofits competing for a piece of the action.</u> The Street Smart talents for niching, positioning, and focusing on strengths can be augmented by the new Social Media. We listen to special pleaders less and are listening to one another more. The key will be to get people who are affected by our issues and concerns and let them carry the message.
- <u>There will be more competition for volunteers and qualified staffs.</u> Street Smart Leaders have always rejected the myth of overdependence on the charismatic leaders and have been great team builders. They

realize that the key is to get individuals with different strengths but shared values AND BELIEFS and link them into a charismatic organization.

- <u>Resources will always be limited</u> but Street Smart Leaders are experts in using the 80/20 rule focusing on the Vital Few (people, media, causes, programs, resources) rather than the "trivial many." They have an eye for the essential things that work –the strengths –and they seem to know how to work around weaknesses.

There will be even more of a premium to translate lofty goals and missions into realizable and measurable goals and objectives. To get the Power Circle to adopt these goals as transformation agents, they know that they will have to keep performing while transforming and getting over setbacks quickly.

One last example to show that "the more things change, the more they are the same." Way back in the 20th century, 1964 to be exact, Marshall McLuhan published <u>Understanding Media: the Extensions of Man</u> and declared that the "electric media" – television, radio, movies and the telephone were now dominant over the printed media. He predicted the rise of the global village ruled by mass media and simultaneous communication would be the constant. The "medium would be the message". To support this global village one would need mass advertisers and mass media with huge budgets and global brands.

Now in the 21st century we have experts who say that the era of mass communciation is over. With the rise of the Internet and the social media, we still have tribes but they are no longer global in scope. Instead we have millions of social, cultural and economic tribes with their unique way of communicating and interacting. The number of alliances is myriad! As a result, ordinary people have the power to lead and make changes. It is no longer a question of dollars.

Human interaction is still the key force in overcoming resistance and speeding change. Social Media may be good in sending out information or creating awareness – the first step in persuasion - - but the next two steps involve trust and action. Usually this requires a social process. We may yearn for frictionless technological solutions but people talking to people – AND REALLY LISTENING TO EACH OTHER – is still the best way to persuade and bring about change.

The new, but really old, success formula for Street Smart nonprofits still applies:

1. Find something remarkable that you do - - provide a unique benefit or solve a special problem; (Your Elevator Speech) Go with your Strengths and work like mad to enhance these strengths. KEEP LISTENING AND KEEP SHARING BELIEFS!

2. Find good people, (The Vital Few) empower them, show appreciation and respect. Form them into your Power Circle - - the Shakers and Makers, the Special experts/Resources, and the Allies and Advocates. And recognize that coaching these Vital Few is an ongoing process.

3. Weave a story around your elevator speech; and get your Power Circle to know it and tell it. GROW ORGANICALLY – from inside out. Have them learn the Planning Process for each program they champion!

4. Practice bottom-up planning (find that unique difference that makes a difference) – and top-down marketing and selling.

5. Connect with your special "tribe" of people, fanatics, or enthusiasts, –who recognize how remarkable you are. They in turn will tell your story to others and the cycle continues and expands.

6. Deliver on your promises - - solve problems or provide benefits for staff, volunteers, donors, partners, etc. The key is resiliency . You experiment your way to success.

Perhaps the best way to end is to remind readers of what we said at the very beginning of the book. Street Smarts is a combination of attitude and practical skills that goes against conventional wisdom and helps you thrive in difficult and dangerous situations. The attitude shift that must be made is to realize that a small nonprofit is just not a smaller version of a big nonprofit. The culture, resources and styles of leadership of the Giants cannot and should not be chiseled down or cobbled to fit the smaller no profits. And of course the practical skills as suggested in the 10 Secrets are special..

The failure to grow is more of a lack of will than resources or capacity. You really have all of the tools you need if you use them with Street Smarts.

# EXERCISE:

After reading about the future issues described by the author and street smart LEADERS look into your own crystal ball and choose the ones that will have most impact on your nonprofit.

Now what can you do about it? Which of the 10 "secrets" can help the most?

# "DESERT ISLAND" BOOK LIST FOR STREET SMART LEADERS

Beaudine, Bob & Dooley, Tom. The Power of Who, Hachette Book, Group 2009.

Bornstein, David & Davis, Susan, Social Entrepreneurship: What everyone needs to Know, Oxford University Press, 2010

Burnett, John J. Nonprofit Marketing, Best Practices, John Wiley, 2007.

Carlson, Richard. Don't Sweat the Small Stuff, MJF Books, 1997.

Crutchfield, Leslier & Grant, Heather McLeod, Forces for Good, Jossey-Bass, 2008.

Drucker, Peter, Managing the NonProfit Organization, Jossey-Bass, 1990.

Drucker, Peter, The Five Most Important Questions You Will Ever Ask About Your NonProfit Organization, Jossey-Bass, 1993.

Firstenberg, Paul B. Managing for Profit in the NonProfit World, The Foundation Center, 1986

Gladwell, Malcolm, David and Goliath, Little Brown, 2013

Horan, Jim, The One Page Business Plan for NonProfit Organizations, The One-Page Business Plan Company, 2007.

Koch, Richard, The 80/20 Rule, Doubleday, 1998.

Kotter, John P. Leading Change, Harvard Business Review Press, 1996.

Levinson, Jay Conrad, Adkins, Frank, Forbes, Chris. Guerrilla Marketing for NonProfits, Entrepreneur Press, 2010.

McRea, Jennifer and Walker, Jeffrey C. The Generosity Network, Deepak Chopra Books, 2013

Miller, Kivi Leroux, The nonprofit Marketing Guide, Jossey-Bass, 2010.

Pallotta, Dan Uncharitable, Tufts University Press, 2008

Ries, Al & Trout, Jack, Positioning: The Battle for Your Mind, McGraw-Hill, 2000.

Sagawa, Shirley & Jospin, Deborah, The Charismatic Organization, Jossey-Bass, 2009.

Scott, David Merman, The New Rules of Marketing and PR. Wiley, 2010.

# "AND IF YOU HAD A LAPTOP AND WIFI ON THAT ISLAND" LIST FOR STREET SMART LEADERS

National Council of Nonprofits (www.councilofnonprofits.org) This site helps leaders navigate the growth and competition facing nonprofits with national trend research and interviews with nonprofit executive leadership. The site also offers resource for training leaders, boards and staff.

The Center for Nonprofit Management (www.cnmsocal. org) For 30 years in Southern California, the Center for Nonprofit Management is the great resource for the non-profit community. By providing assistance in a variety of areas, the Center has supported thousands of organizations as they meet the needs of their communities. Check out our list of the best blogs for non-profit leaders.

For Advice:

1. Nonprofit Conversation (www.nonprofitconversation. blogspot.com) Bunnie Riedel's blog shares discussions on nonprofit success.

2. Nonprofit CMS (www.nonprofitcms.org/blog/) Nonprofit CMS educates nonprofit leaders on the details of web de-sign, technology, and content management.

3.  The Nonprofit Blog (www.ruthellenrubin.com/polBlog.cfm) Ruthellen Rubin & Associates writes this blog that offers resources and expertise for nonprofit leaders.

4.  Trina Isakson (http://trinaisakson.com/) Trina's blog is about nonprofit capacity, community development, and more.

5.  Christopher Scott (http://christopherscottblog.typepad. com/) Christopher Scott is a nonprofit leader helping to develop other nonprofit leaders.

    For Grants and Fundraising:

1.  Big Thinking on Small Grants (http://janisfoster.blogspot. com/) Think big about your grants with this blog.

2.  Future Fundraising Now (www.futurefundraisingnow.com/ future-fundraising/) Future Fundraising Now discusses how to do fundraising right.

3.  Friends Asking Amy: (www.friendsaskingamy.com/). Amy Braiterman discusses fundraising tips on this blog.

4.  Get Fully Funded Blog (http://getfullyfundedblog.com/) Sandy Rees offers inspiration for fundraising.

5.  A Small Change (www.asmallchange.net/) A Small Change makes sense of fundraising for nonprofits.

6.  Fired-Up Fundraising (www.gailperry.com/) Gail Perry's blog will help you get fired up about fundraising.

For Social Media:

1. Beth's Blog (www.bethkanter.org/)Beth's Blog discusses how networked nonprofits are using social media to power change.

2. Netwits Think Tank: (www.netwitsthinktank.com/)This blog offers an online resource for nonprofits using social media, Internet marketing, and online fundraising.

3. Socialize Your Cause: (www.socializeyourcause.org/blog/) Socialize Your Cause will help you bring social media to your cause.

4. Socialbrite: (www.socialbrite.org/)Read Socialbrite to find social tools for social change.

5. John Haydon: (www.johnhaydon.com/)John Haydon's blog is all about social media marketing for nonprofits.

For Research:

1. The National Center for Charitable Statistics: (http://nccsdataweb.urban.org/) It contains the Nonprofit FAQ and provides answers and tips for over 125 nonprofit topics.

2. Greenlights: (www.greenlights.org) Online library with a variety of templates, how-to's, research and tips on nonprofit best practices

3. Nonprofit Resource Center: (www.nprcenter.org) Provides resources and improve the management of nonprofit organizations, primarily within California but is a great resource anywhere.

# ABOUT THE AUTHOR

William A. (Bill) Mindak has spent his academic career either starting up nonprofits or helping them go through critical transitioning periods. He was the Director of Tulane's Business School Executive MBA program. He has served as a consultant to Tulane's Medical Center, the Volunteers of America, Credit Union National Association (CUNA), and the Lighthouse of the Blind. He's conducted workshops for the American Heart Association, the American Lung Association, and the March of Dimes. Currently he's working with the Odyssey House of Louisiana and the Wellness Center of Louisiana. He is Professor Emeritus of Marketing at the A. B. Freeman School of Business and consultant to the Goldring International Institute.

www.ingramcontent.com/pod-product-compliance
Lightning Source LLC
Chambersburg PA
CBHW051517170526
45165CB00002B/504